# His Spirit is with us

## A project-based programme
## on communion

Leslie J. Francis & Diane Drayson

kevin
**mayhew**

*His Spirit is with us* contains material revised from *Bread for all God's family* by Leslie J. Francis and Diane Drayson.
Leominster, Gracewing, 1997. ISBN 0 85244 283 1

First published in 2003 by

KEVIN MAYHEW LTD
Buxhall, Stowmarket, Suffolk IP14 3BW
Email: info@kevinmayhewltd.com

KINGSGATE PUBLISHING INC
1000 Pannell Street, Suite G, Columbia, MO 65201
Email: sales@kingsgatepublishing.com

9 8 7 6 5 4 3 2 1 0

ISBN 1 84417 018 7
Catalogue No. 1500568

Cover design by Angela Selfe
Cover illustration by Phillip Vernon
Edited by Katherine Laidler
Typeset by Louise Selfe
Printed in Great Britain

# Contents

Foreword   5

Introduction   7

Resources   17

1   Getting to know you *The Lord be with you*   18

2   Ways with water *Collect for Purity*   22

3   Barrier builders *Confession*   26

4   The mender *Absolution*   30

5   Making music *Glory to God*   34

6   Your clergy *Collect*   38

7   Hear all about it *Ministry of the Word*   42

8   Follow the signs *We believe in God*   46

9   Meeting Jesus of Nazareth *We believe in Jesus Christ*   50

10   Windy day *We believe in the Holy Spirit*   54

11   Between friends *Invitation to prayer*   58

12   Meeting the Church *Prayer for the Church*   62

13   Around the world *Prayer for the world*   66

14   Meet the neighbours *Prayer for our neighbourhood*   70

15   Sick call *Prayer for the suffering*   74

16   Light and life *Prayer for the departed*   78

17   Say it with hands *Peace*   82

18   Shopping spree *Preparation of the gifts*   86

19   Bird watching *Preface to the Eucharistic Prayer*   90

20   Journey into space *Holy, holy, holy Lord*   94

21   Wedding reception *Institution Narrative*   98

22   Bread and wine *Acclamation*   102

23   Carnival time *Thanksgiving and Doxology*   106

24   Picnic time *Lord's Prayer*   110

25   Fair shares *Breaking the bread*   114

26   Pilgrim way *Invitation*   118

27   Birthday invitation *We do not presume*   122

28   Known by name *Administration*   126

29   Come dancing *After communion*   130

30   Rainbows *Blessing*   134

31   Helping hands *Dismissal*   138

Take-home sheets   143

# About the authors

Leslie Francis is an Anglican priest with experience in parochial ministry and classroom teaching. Currently he is Professor of Practical Theology at the University of Wales, Bangor, non-stipendiary priest in the Ogwen deanery, and Director of the Welsh National Centre for Religious Education.

Diane Drayson is a primary school teacher and professional author and editor with considerable experience in writing educational and church-related material. Currently she teaches in Oxfordshire.

# Foreword

This programme of Christian education is part of a wider initiative pioneered by the Welsh National Centre for Religious Education to enhance the ministry of the Churches among children. We believe ministry among children to be a matter of crucial importance for the Churches today. Every congregation needs to challenge and call out vocations to this ministry.

Some Churches now recognise and authorise this specialist ministry among children in much the same way as they train, recognise, and authorise the ministry of preaching. Here in the Welsh National Centre for Religious Education we have developed a distance learning Certificate of Higher Education in Ministry among Children which can be completed by part-time study. Further information about this programme can be obtained by writing to the authors at the address below.

*His Spirit is with us* also arises from two deeply held personal commitments: commitment to eucharistic worship at the centre of the Christian life and commitment to children at the centre of eucharistic worship. We are grateful to those congregations with whom we have worked and worshipped for their part in shaping our thinking and practice; to the many clergy, teachers, Sunday school leaders and diocesan advisers who have offered advice; and to Anne Rees and Susan Thomas who shaped the manuscript.

Leslie J. Francis and Diane Drayson
Welsh National Centre for Religious Education
Normal Site
University of Wales, Bangor
Gwynedd LL57 2PX
Wales, UK

# Introduction

*His Spirit is with us* is a companion to the illustrated communion book *The Lord is Here!* It provides a project-based programme of Christian education based on the communion service, which aims to develop understanding of the eucharist and to promote a positive attitude towards worship. This introduction contains six sections.

The section **Why?** explains the principles upon which the book is based. It answers the question: Why does this book follow its particular pattern?

The section **How?** gives details of the layout of each chapter. It answers the question: How can the resources be used?

The section **Where?** suggests different contexts in which the book can be used. It answers the question: Where can children's work take place?

The section **What?** gives examples from the programme, showing how it can be integrated into the worship of the church. It answers the question: What will this approach be like in practice?

The section **Who?** explores the privilege and importance of ministry among children. It answers the question: Who can be involved in this programme?

The section **When?** suggests different ways of fitting these units in with the ongoing programme of children's work in the church. It answers the question: When can this programme be used?

## WHY?

The eucharist has come to play an increasingly important part in Anglican worship. The parish communion and the family communion are the key Sunday services in many Anglican churches.

At the same time attendance at the Sunday service has come to play an increasingly important part in the Christian education and nurture of young Anglicans. Children are present for all or part of the main Sunday communion service in many Anglican churches.

There are good theological and educational principles behind both of these movements. *His Spirit is with us* accepts these principles and offers a programme designed to put these principles into practice. The programme is committed to all-age participation, concrete images and project learning.

### All-age participation

All-age learning and worship recognises that all individuals, children and adults alike, come with different experiences, different needs and different ways of expressing themselves. All-age learning and worship needs to take these differences seriously.

All-age learning and worship also recognises that individual members of the church learn best from each other. Learning is a two-way process. Children learn from adults and adults learn from children. They are travelling together on a shared pilgrimage and are able to enrich and resource each other for the journey.

Because individuals differ so greatly there are times when their learning and worship can best take place in sub-groups able to focus on specialist needs. Workshops or worship sessions for children may provide examples of such sub-groups. Because individuals learn from others' differences there are also times when their learning and worship can best take place together.

### Concrete images

The communion service, as celebrated in Anglican churches today, uses a liturgy which has been carefully and skilfully crafted. Each component of the service has its roots in history, scripture and tradition. For the communion service to come alive to children and adults alike this liturgy needs to be made accessible to them. Nor can it be assumed that all worshippers, children and adults alike, are familiar with the history, scripture and tradition known so well by those who wrote the service books.

The aim of this programme is to unwrap the complex religious language of the liturgy and to reveal the fundamental basic and concrete images which underpin this language. Each section takes just one concrete image and shows how this image relates to and illuminates one part of the communion service. For example, the section on 'the wind' helps us to grasp how this image held the key for both the Hebrew-speaking Old Testament and the Greek-speaking New Testament to talk about God as Holy Spirit.

The concrete images underpinning religious language provide a crucial aid not only for children but for adults as well. After all, religious language is not meaningful until we have grasped the reality to which it points and from which it is derived.

### Project learning

Language acquires its significance from being grounded in human experience. Project learning structures the opportunities for adults and children to experience the concrete images underpinning religious language. Adults and children are encouraged to explore these images at their own level and at their own pace. The fruits of such exploration are then to be shared.

For example, the section on 'the wind' suggests a wide range of practical activities through which children and adults can be helped to experience the wind and to reflect on these experiences. Through their experiences they are encouraged to explore the theological idea of God as Spirit. Then these theological insights can be grounded in the celebration of communion.

## HOW?

*His Spirit is with us* contains 31 distinct chapters. Each chapter identifies a clear concrete image and relates this image to a basic part of the communion service. Although these are printed in the order in which they may be encountered in the communion service, they need not be used consecutively. Each chapter is independent. Chapters can be used in any order, depending on what is appropriate and needful.

In each chapter, specific suggestions are offered for children's activities and for all-age projects. Clear guidance is given for integrating this learning within the celebration of communion. To achieve these ends each chapter is divided into four sections:

- key aims
- worship resources
- children's workshops
- celebrating together

### Key aims

The key aims set out the intentions of the project programme. These aims include the rationale for the children's workshops, the all-age project and the worship celebration together. At the end of each project and celebration the leaders should assess how far the aims have been realised.

### Worship resources

The section on worship resources provides six headings.

**Reference to communion service** This introduction to each chapter discusses the part of the communion service which the project theme illuminates and provides background information for those leading the activities and celebration.

**Picture** This section illustrates the way in which the pictures in *The Lord is Here!* contribute to shaping the project theme.

**Bible story** The passages from Scripture presented in this section illustrate how the project activities and the key images in the communion service relate to the Bible. This material may be used directly with children and adults or adapted by the leaders.

**Hymns and songs** Hymns and songs have been indicated as relevant to each project theme. It is important to recognise that hymns known best to children from school hymn books are unlikely to be known by many adult worshippers, while the church's traditional hymns are now relatively unknown to many children. Consequently, churches may need to introduce 'school' hymns to their adult congregation and 'church' hymns to their children. These hymns and songs are selected from *Come and Praise* (volumes 1 and 2), *Ancient and Modern New Standard, Hymns Old and New: New Anglican Edition, Complete Anglican Hymns Old and New*, and *Hymns and Songs for Assembly*. Three hymns and songs have been chosen from each of these five books for every project theme. Many of the hymns and songs are also published in the other books and can be traced through use of their indexes.

**Bible readings** Some churches may wish to focus the whole celebration of the eucharist on a specific project theme. When this is the case, three readings from Scripture have been identified to reflect this theme. The controlling reading, marked with an asterisk, generally also features in the expanded Bible story.

**Prayer** A collect has been composed for each project to sum up the worship theme. This may be used in the eucharist alongside the three Bible readings.

## Children's workshops

The section on children's workshops provides five headings. For each unit select ideas from these headings. You may choose to use an idea from each part; you may choose to use an idea from only three parts. Select those that best suit the needs and interests of your participants.

**Ice-breaker** There are many different ways of initiating each project theme within children's workshops. While this section suggests one idea for each of them, experienced teachers may prefer to use their own ideas.

**Activities** The activities suggest a range of things to do or to make. These activities are best suited for a single, relatively brief session. Leaders may wish to select one of these activities for the whole group, or work on different activities with different groups and then share the results.

**Projects** The projects also suggest a range of things to do or to make. These projects are best in situations when the theme is developed over a series of sessions or through a whole day workshop. Again leaders may wish to select one of these projects for the whole group, or work on different projects with different groups and then share the result.

**Discussion starters** Project activities should be used as a springboard for reflection and discussion. This section suggests some topics which may be developed as appropriate by the teachers and leaders.

**Dance/drama** Dance and drama are powerful ways for children to explore feelings and ideas which they can share creatively with the adult congregation. While suggestions are included for each theme, teachers and leaders may wish to use them only when time and space are available.

## Celebrating together

The section on celebrating together provides suggestions for the worship service. It contains three headings.

**All-age involvement** The sections on all-age involvement suggest ways in which the whole congregation, adults as well as children, can be involved in the same kind of project learning as promoted through the children's workshops. The fruits of the all-age projects can, therefore, be placed alongside the fruits of the children's workshops to be discussed and interpreted in a similar fashion. Sometimes churches may decide to employ the ideas provided for the all-age projects without operating the parallel activities within children's workshops.

Generally the all-age projects benefit from forward planning so that regular worshippers can come to the service prepared with ideas and practical resources.

**The service** This section suggests ways in which the children's activities and the all-age projects can most effectively be integrated within the celebration of eucharist. Often this may involve introducing activities or discussion and displaying project work at the point in the service where the concrete image most appropriately illuminates the language of the liturgy. For example, project activities on the theme of 'the wind' can be employed most effectively in association with the third section of the Creed when the worshipping community confesses faith in God as Holy Spirit. The extent and frequency with which this approach is appropriate will vary from church to church.

**Display** The link between project learning and the communion service is established by displaying the fruits of the children's workshops and all-age projects in church. It is often helpful to leave this work on display after the service in which it has been celebrated. This section suggests a brief form of words to interpret the display for children and adults. Leaders may provide more extensive display headings of their own.

## Take-home sheets

For each unit two take-home sheets are provided in a form which can be easily photocopied. These can be found at the back of the book. The take-home sheets are for groups which wish to continue the learning activities at home, or to communicate to parents the content of the sessions. Each unit is complete without these sheets; their use is optional.

Two different types of sheets are included for each session. The **Worship resource (Celebrating at home)** contains material that is also included in the leaders' notes. This reinforces the children's learning and informs the parents of what the children are doing. In addition there is an activity for each unit that can be done at home with the family so that the learning extends to the home. The **Activity sheet** is a separate project to do at home, an activity to interest the children while it reinforces the theme of the unit.

Choose for yourself how to use these sheets, according to the needs of your group. Be prepared to change from unit to unit. For some units you may prefer to use neither sheet. For other units you may prefer just one or both sheets. It is your choice.

You can also choose when to use the sheets. The **Activity sheet** could be sent home before the unit begins in order to stimulate the children's thinking and to prepare them for the learning that will take place. Alternatively it could be sent home at the end of the unit in order to extend the children's learning. The **Worship resource** should be sent home at the end of the unit. Churches which spend several weeks on each unit may prefer to send the **Activity sheet** home at the end of the first week, and then send the **Worship resource** home when the unit is completed.

## WHERE?

Many factors influence how local churches organise their children's work, including patterns of Sunday services, numbers of children, willingness of teachers and leaders, and availability of buildings. It is increasingly recognised that the key to effective work among children requires regular contact with the adult congregation. This can be achieved in a range of ways, including weekly withdrawal classes, a monthly pattern of Sunday school and family services, weekday evening sessions, project days and co-operation with church schools. *His Spirit is with us* is appropriate for all these contexts but will be used differently in each setting.

### Withdrawal classes

Some churches have children present for part of the main communion service each Sunday. Either they come to the first part of the Ministry of the Word and withdraw before the sermon, or they begin their own classes separately and join the adults for the Ministry of the Sacrament, at the Offertory or the Fraction. These withdrawal classes are likely to be relatively short and it is necessary to focus the lesson with care.

If children are brought into the service for the Ministry of the Sacrament, it is important that they feel welcomed by the adult congregation. The Peace can express this welcome most helpfully. If the children are introduced at the Fraction, rather than the Offertory, it may be possible to defer the Peace to this part of the service, where it is placed in the Roman rite.

*His Spirit is with us* can be used in two different ways when withdrawal classes are held. Some churches may decide to introduce a new project theme each week. They will select one or two key activities for the children to enjoy and then share these activities with the whole congregation later in the service. Other churches may decide to spend several weeks exploring one project theme before sharing it with the congregation. When the project is ready to share with the whole congregation it is an appropriate time to share the all-age project as well.

## Sunday school and family services

Some churches operate their children's work most Sunday mornings separately from the main service, but once a month integrate children and adults for a family communion service. This model has several advantages. Once a month it lets the main communion service be more child-centred, while on the other Sundays it lets the adults tailor a service appropriate to their needs and allows more time for the children's work in their own classes.

If a monthly pattern is employed one theme can be developed more fully over three weeks. For the family communion service the children's project work can be displayed in the church during the previous week, the theme of the service can be developed around the project work, using the suggested collect and readings, and full use can be made of the ideas offered in the sections 'all-age project' and 'the service'.

## Weekday evening sessions

Some churches organise their children's work through weekday evening sessions. These churches either expect the children to be present at the main Sunday morning service each week, or arrange a special family communion service once a month.

Either a new project theme can be introduced each week or one theme can be developed over several sessions. If the church holds a monthly family communion service, the weekday evening sessions can prepare for these services, with dance, drama, music and display materials. Full use can be made in the monthly service of the ideas offered in the sections 'all-age project' and 'the service'. If the church does not hold a monthly family communion service, display the children's work in church week by week and enable the children to contribute something from their project work most Sundays.

## Project days

Some churches do all or part of their children's work through project days or project half-days on a Saturday, during school holidays or at half-term. Project days permit a theme to be explored in depth and may include a wide range of craft, dance, drama and music, as well as special features like outings and field trips. Project days need to relate closely to the main communion service on the following Sunday, when the children's work can be integrated as they celebrate the climax of their project with the adult congregation around the eucharist.

## Church schools

Some churches have a close link with a local church school. *His Spirit is with us* is ideally suited for church schools which want to link the general curriculum with the worship of the church. Teachers will identify many ways in which these projects can be promoted across the curriculum and how they can enable individual classes or the whole school to contribute constructively towards the Sunday communion service in church, as well as to school eucharists.

## WHAT?

One part of the communion service is the prayer for the Church and the world. Children can understand this in terms of the theme 'my neighbourhood', a topic or project which is often covered by the primary school. Children of different ages and different abilities are all able in their own way to contribute to a study of their local neighbourhood and the people who live and work there. A topic like this utilises all aspects of the primary school curriculum and becomes part of a programme of Christian nurture when the topic is related to the eucharist. The children's understanding of the prayer for the Church and the world is enriched. The church building is where the project is displayed, and the eucharist offers the project to God. The sacrament is where secular and sacred meet.

Another example is provided by the third section of the Creed where the worshipping community states belief in the Holy Spirit. The link is provided so clearly by the languages of the Bible, Hebrew and Greek, in which the same word signifies both wind and spirit, making the wind a primary Christian image for the Holy Spirit.

In developing projects about the Holy Spirit, we can explore the many facets of the wind. We can make kites and visit the park to fly them. We can make windmills and take a trip to see one. We can blow up balloons and hold a party with them. We can pretend that we are out on the mountain struggling against the gale, or on some tropical island basking in a warm breeze. We can dance the dance of leaves caught up in the wind. We can write stories and poems about the wind and paint pictures. By doing these things we can learn about the mysterious movement of the Holy Spirit. And along the way we can encounter extracts from Scripture, as well as modern and traditional hymns about the Holy Spirit.

Then we can take the results of our project to church on Sunday. A hot air balloon can be hung from the pulpit. A windmill can be stood on the font. Balloons can be suspended above the pews and let down at the end of the service. Our drawings, poems and stories can be mounted and displayed. The photographs of our visit to the park and the windmill can be shared with those who come to worship alongside us. Our dance and drama about the wind can be presented before the whole worshipping community as that community comes together to celebrate its faith in the Christ of the eucharist.

The children enjoy their topic and project work on the wind. Their families and friends enjoy seeing their work contribute to the eucharist. Most of all, when the third section of the Creed is recited the project work on the wind points to the mysterious wind-like quality of God the Holy Spirit.

## WHO?

The work of ministry among children is a matter of crucial importance for the Church today. Every congregation needs to challenge and call out vocations for this ministry.

In today's Church some people will want to set aside time to be trained for a ministry among children. Ministry among children is no less important than the ministry of preaching. Some professional programmes are now available to lead to a Certificate of Higher Education in Ministry among Children. Some churches now recognise and authorise this specialist ministry in much the same way as they train, recognise, and authorise the ministry of preaching.

In today's Church other people will be prepared and equipped to contribute in a variety of ways to the church's ministry among children on a more casual basis. The ministry of such volunteers needs to be well organised and properly integrated into the local church's overall strategy. Congregations will contain skilled people who are able to contribute to this ministry in a variety of ways and sometimes on a one-off basis. For example, there may be skilled wine-makers in the congregation who would love to share their enthusiasm and skills with children when they explore the ways in which the wine of eucharist brings to God both the fruit of the vine and the work of human hands.

It is important to remember the great trust and responsibility placed in the hands of all those invited to share in the Church's work among children and young people. Each church is required to have an agreed Child Protection Policy in place, and needs to have the official police check run on everyone who is engaged in contact with children on behalf of the church, whether they carry out this ministry as paid employees or as volunteers. Further information on the recognised procedures should be obtainable from the appropriate church officers.

## WHEN?

*His Spirit is with us* suggests separate projects for 31 sections in the communion service, in order to develop understanding of the eucharist and to promote a positive attitude towards worship. The barrier between the religious and the secular begins to dissolve and children begin to feel at home in church. Adults, too, find their understanding of the church's worship enriched.

For some churches *His Spirit is with us* will integrate into their on-going programme of Sunday school work, Christian nurture and all-age learning and worship. Others may decide to use it to help the whole congregation take a full part in confirmation training, or in a programme of preparation for admission to communion.

The 31 themes will not necessarily be used in the order in which they are published. Churches may prefer to vary the order to suit local needs, to integrate with work going on in local schools, or to coincide with the rhythm of the Church's year. Nor is it assumed that every church will want to use all 31 sections.

For churches which select 10 key projects, *His Spirit is with us* provides resources for a full term's work. For churches which use all 31 projects at the rate of one per week, *His Spirit is with us* provides resources for a year's work of three 10-week terms. For churches which pace the projects more slowly and explore each theme in greater depth over three or four sessions, culminating in a monthly family communion service, *His Spirit is with us* provides resources for a three-year cycle of work.

Whichever method of working is adopted, *His Spirit is with us* is a programme of Christian nurture which offers a vision for the Church's future and a firm commitment to children, project learning and all-age worship. The next step is simply to choose a topic, any topic between 1 and 31, and to put the vision to the test.

# Resources

# 1

# Getting to know you

## KEY AIMS

- To help children and adults explore the greeting 'The Lord be with you'
- To help the children get to know each other
- To help the children tell the congregation about themselves
- To help the children feel valued by the congregation

## WORSHIP RESOURCES

### Reference to communion service

*The Lord be with you*

'The Lord be with you' is an ancient form of greeting. At the opening of the communion service the greeting establishes relationships between all the individuals in the congregation and the president, ready for them to start the service together. By making the response together, the people acknowledge from the start that each one of them counts as an important member of the congregation.

### Picture

The picture shows two children getting to know each other as they throw their colourful ball to and fro. They are clearly having fun.

### Bible story

*Jesus chooses 12 friends* (Mark 3:13-19)

When Jesus began his work he chose 12 people to be his close friends. Jesus wanted to get to know these 12 friends very well; and he wanted them to learn about his way of life by listening to what he said and watching what he did. Jesus' 12 friends were called Peter and Andrew, James and John, Philip, Bartholomew, Matthew, Thomas, James, Thaddaeus, Simon and Judas. Jesus gave some of them nicknames, which described the sort of people they were. Peter he called 'the Rock'; James and John he called 'Sons of Thunder'. We, too, are called to be Jesus' close friends. He knows each of us by name. 'The Lord be with you!'

## Hymns and songs

*Come and Praise*
Guess how I feel (89)
He gave me eyes so I could see (18)
One more step along the world I go (47) ✓

*Hymns Ancient and Modern New Standard*
Just as I am without one plea (246)
Lord of all good, our gifts we bring to thee (393)
Lord God, your love has called us here (489)

*Hymns Old and New: New Anglican Edition*
It's me, it's me, it's me, O Lord (256)
May the mind of Christ my Saviour (334)
The King is among us (483)

*Complete Anglican Hymns Old and New*
A wiggly, waggly worm (777)
Do you ever wish you could fly like a bird (792)
It's me, it's me, it's me, O Lord (838)

*Hymns and Songs for Assembly*
If I were a butterfly (47)
I'm special because God has loved me (56)
There are hundreds of sparrows (109)

## Bible readings

Old Testament – Ruth 2:1-4
New Testament – 1 Corinthians 1:1-4
*Gospel – Mark 3:13-19

## Prayer

All-loving God,
you know each one of us by name,
and you love us all.
Help us to feel your presence with us,
and to grow closer to each other;
through Jesus Christ our Lord.

## CHILDREN'S WORKSHOP

### Ice-breaker

Sit with the children in a circle on the floor. Ask them to identify themselves (whatever name they are known by at home or by their friends) and to say something about themselves, like 'I am Jim and I am good at football.' Respond to each, 'Hello, Jim, you're good at football', to show that you have noticed them and take an interest in them.

### Activities

- Invite the children to make large name badges on card. These badges could include information about the children, such as favourite food, favourite game, current ambition, and most admired person.

- Help the children to organise key information about themselves to share with the church congregation – for example, their age, height, colour of eyes and hair, length of span, the street, area or village where they live, number of brothers and sisters, weight, favourite food, etc. To present this information, prepare a large sheet of paper before the session. Write headings along the top (for example, age, height). Write the children's names down the left-hand side. Rule your paper into sections. The children can either write directly on your poster or can write on small pieces of paper to paste on. Where possible make the information pictorial – for example, coloured squares to indicate colour of eyes.

- Before your session (perhaps with the help of some of the children) make a large poster of a bus, with one window space for each child. Ask the children to draw portraits of themselves to paste in the windows of the bus. Write each child's name under the appropriate window. The name of the church can also be written on the side of the bus.

## Projects

- Find large sheets of paper, bigger than the children. Ask the children to draw round each other as they lie on the floor on the paper. These outlines can be coloured in with poster paints or turned into collages with remnants of wallpaper and glue. Write the child's name on each picture.

- Make twelve large figures to represent the twelve disciples and name each of the figures. These could be cardboard outlines (cut from large boxes) with each body part cut separately and attached with large split pins to make it movable. Add remnants of material as clothes. Paste on wool for hair. Use accessories to remind you of the disciples' occupations or of key Bible stories – for example, John with a fishing net and Andrew with five loaves and seven fish. If you can store these figures you may find them useful for future displays – for example, Christmas – changing clothes where necessary.

- Make 'Meet me' zigzag books, one for each child to display in church. Page 1 could be a photograph; page 2 could be a description including age, height, eye and hair colour, etc.; page 3 could be information about favourite activities, and so on. If zigzag books are made, they can be easily displayed and compared.

## Discussion starters

- The different ways people greet each other: the wave through the window, the handshake, the kiss, the words they use
- What do I notice about other children in church?
- What do I want to tell the congregation about myself?

## Dance/drama

Devise a dance to symbolise the way all are brought together through the eucharist. First work out a movement which symbolises this togetherness (for example, standing in a circle with hands joined and arms raised) and a place for this to happen (the centre of the room or the communion table). Next ask the children to space themselves out round the edges of the room or corners of the church to perform isolated dance movement. Explain that you will beat a drum five times. At the first drum beat they are to begin to move closer and to look at each other and copy each other's movements. At the second drum beat they should move together into a large circle, dancing on the spot. At the third drum beat a leader says, 'The Lord be with you' and all reply, 'And also with you.' At this point they hold hands and side-step clockwise. At the fourth drum beat they move into the centre with raised arms and remain together, still, until the final beat. Practise this with appropriate music.

## CELEBRATING TOGETHER

### All-age involvement

Invite all members of the congregation to make a small poster about themselves at home, and to include whatever information they may wish to share. Suggest including an up-to-date photograph and some photographs from earlier stages in their lives. Display these posters around the church before the service begins.

### The service

Before the opening greeting takes place, explain the significance of that greeting. Invite the congregation to walk round the church looking at the display. The children may describe their activities and lead the opening greeting. If the children have prepared a dance this can be shared immediately after the greeting to illustrate its significance.

### Display

The communion service begins with the greeting 'The Lord be with you' and it means with each one of us. So here we are to introduce ourselves.

# Ways with water

## KEY AIMS

- To help children and adults explore the Collect for Purity
- To help the children recall the importance of water in everyday life
- To help the children recognise the place of water in baptism
- To help the children appreciate our need for God's cleansing

## WORSHIP RESOURCES

### Reference to communion service

*Collect for Purity*

At the opening of the communion service, the Collect for Purity emphasises that we are not worthy to approach God in the eucharist unless God first takes the initiative for that meeting. This prayer for cleansing at the beginning of the eucharist reminds us of the symbolism of water in the Sacrament of Baptism at the very beginning of our Christian way of life.

### Picture

The picture shows a young person being baptised in the flowing water of the river. Other people have interrupted their journey by the river bank to witness this baptism.

### Bible story

*Philip baptises the Ethiopian official* (Acts 8:26-40)

When people wanted to join the early disciples and apostles as members of the Church, they asked to be baptised. The Ethiopian official was someone like this. He had read about God in the Bible and Philip had told him the good news about Jesus. The Ethiopian official made up his mind that he wanted to join Jesus' followers. He said to Philip, 'Here is water: what is there to prevent my being baptised?' Philip asked him to speak aloud his faith in Jesus. He replied, 'I believe that Jesus Christ is the Son of God.' Philip led him down into the water and baptised him. He became a member of the Church. We, too, become members of the Church when we are baptised in water. We remember our baptism when we come to worship God in the eucharist and when we ask God to 'cleanse the thoughts of our hearts'.

## Hymns and songs

*Come and Praise*
All creatures of our God and King (7)
Have you heard the raindrops drumming on the roof tops? (2)
Waves are beating on the shore (84)

*Hymns Ancient and Modern New Standard*
Breathe on me, Breath of God (157)
Christ, when for us you were baptised (442)
Praise and thanksgiving be to our Creator (506)

*Hymns Old and New: New Anglican Edition*
Be thou my guardian and my guide (55)
Glorious things of thee are spoken (158)
Purify my heart (428)

*Complete Anglican Hymns Old and New*
At the dawning of creation (52)
The wise man built his house upon the rock (897)
You can drink it, swim in it (917)

*Hymns and Songs for Assembly*
All over the world the Spirit is moving (4)
As the deer pants for the water (8)
Father welcomes all his children (25)

## Bible readings

Old Testament – 2 Kings 5:1-14
*New Testament – Acts 8:35-39
Gospel – Matthew 28:16-20

## Prayer

Almighty God,
you make us clean
with the water of baptism
and accept us into your Church.
Send your Holy Spirit on us
to cleanse the thoughts of our hearts
and to make us ready to worship you;
through Jesus Christ our Lord.

## CHILDREN'S WORKSHOP

### Ice-breaker

Find a very large water jug or container (perhaps there is one in church used for filling the font) and a large bowl or baby bath. Ask the children to look carefully as you slowly empty the jug, to watch the light play on the running water and to listen to the sounds. Ask them to describe what they see and hear. Invite the children to dip one finger in the water to feel the water and to hold their finger up to dry. Ask them to describe what they feel. Fill enough small plastic beakers with chilled water for

each child to have one and ask them to sniff the water and to sip it slowly. Ask them to describe what they smell, taste and feel as they drink.

### Activities
- Make a collage of all the different uses of water, using magazine pictures of baths, showers, drink bottles, sinks, washing machines, car washes, etc.
- Make a water wheel from a circle of stout card. Cut one-third of the way into the centre at regular intervals around the circle. Fold these sections at right-angles to the rest of the circle. Along each fold line, cut to the half-way point and then fold half of the section back (like a step). Place a hole in the centre and use a pencil as a spindle. Operate the wheel by placing it under gently running water.
- Experience the power of water to clean. Wash some dishes or tea towels or a dirty car.

### Projects
- Place two flowers in identical containers: fill one with water and leave the other empty. Place beans on two sheets of blotting paper: keep one moist and the other dry. Observe the different effects.
- Make a picture of a baptism scene depicting vicar, font, child, parents, godparents, countless onlookers, etc. Each person could be drawn separately, cut out and pasted on to a large sheet to make the scene. (You will first need to decide with the children the size and actions of each figure so that they fit together.) Set alongside this another picture of baptism by total immersion – for example, Philip baptising the Ethiopian official or a modern scene from a Baptist church.
- Make a model of a font, using clay or papier mâché.

### Discussion starters
- Water, rivers, streams, wells
- Make a list of all the different uses of water
- Imagine a world without any water
- What happens at a baptism service?
- Ask the children to bring their baptism certificates and to talk about them

### Dance/drama
Act out a baptism service, using a doll or teddy bear, with children taking the part of the priest, the parents, the godparents, friends, etc.

# CELEBRATING TOGETHER

## All-age involvement

Invite all members of the congregation to bring along photographs, paintings or magazine pictures about water: the beach, a bath, a waterfall, a stream, washing, drinking, etc. Display these pictures thematically. Buzz groups, one to each theme, can list words that come to mind as they look at the display.

## The service

Immediately after the opening greeting, invite the congregation to think about the Collect for Purity and the significance of water. Draw attention to the activity work and invite the congregation to recall the significance of their own baptisms in water. If the children have prepared drama based on a baptism service this can be presented immediately after the New Testament reading.

## Display

The Collect for Purity reminds us that we need God to prepare and cleanse us before we come to worship. Each time we say this prayer we are reminded of the water of our baptisms.

# 3

# Barrier builders

## KEY AIMS

- To help children and adults explore the need for confession and forgiveness
- To help the children explore the function of physical barriers
- To help the children understand how they build up barriers, between themselves and other people and between themselves and God
- To help the children explore the standards of conduct God wants of them

## WORSHIP RESOURCES

### Reference to communion service

*Confession*

Sin is the barrier between people and God, which breaks down proper relationships between them. The Confession invites us to review those barriers which we build between ourselves and other people and between ourselves and God. We say that we are sorry about the barriers we build and we ask God to forgive us.

### Picture

The picture shows conflicts which break down proper relationships between people. One picture illustrates children who have abandoned their game of football for a fight. The second picture reminds us that adults can experience similar feelings of anger.

### Bible story

*Jesus' summary of the law* (Matthew 22:35-40)

In the Old Testament God gave Moses the Ten Commandments. The people were instructed to keep these laws and to base their lives on them. In the New Testament Jesus summed up all Ten Commandments as two key laws. Jesus said, 'Love the Lord your God with all your heart, with all your soul, with all your mind. That is the greatest commandment. It comes first. The second is like it. Love your neighbour as yourself.' When we break these great commandments we build up barriers between God and ourselves. That is why we need to confess our sins so that God may forgive us and remove the barriers.

## Hymns and songs

*Come and Praise* _EH_
The King of love my shepherd is (54)  _457_
When I needed a neighbour were you there? (65)
You can build a wall around you (91)

*Hymns Ancient and Modern New Standard*
Forgive our sins as we forgive (362)  _66 EH_
Jesus, whose all-redeeming love (383)
O for a heart to praise my God (230)  _74_

*Hymns Old and New: New Anglican Edition* _EH_
Dear Lord and Father of mankind (106)  _353_
Forgive us our sins as we forgive (141)
Forty days and forty nights (144)  _67_

*Complete Anglican Hymns Old and New*
Father welcomes all his children (797)
Jesus went away to the desert, praying (852)
Lord, you've promised, through your Son (864)

*Hymns and Songs for Assembly*
Can you build a wall around you (134)
Father welcomes all his children (3)
God forgave my sin in Jesus' name (33)

## Bible readings

Old Testament – Exodus 20:1-17
New Testament – 1 Corinthians 11:27-29
*Gospel – Matthew 22:35-40

## Prayer

Merciful God,
you sent your Son
to break down the barriers of sin.
Make us truly sorry for our misdeeds
and give us your pardon and peace,
that we may serve you
in newness of life;
through Jesus Christ our Lord.

## CHILDREN'S WORKSHOP

### Ice-breaker

When the children arrive get them to build a wall with cardboard boxes
or hassocks from the church, so that there is a real barrier in the room.
End up with some children one side of the barrier and some the other
side. Talk about the effect that the barrier has on the room and how it
gets in the way of their relationships with each other. Then make a list of
other barriers they know in their neighbourhood, for example:

- the barrier outside the school gate prevents children from rushing into the road; it also makes crossing the road more difficult
- the barrier alongside the fast road makes the traffic safer; it also means that pedestrians have to go by a long way round
- the level crossing gates protect you from the train; they also sometimes make you late
- the less concrete barriers like 'no entry' signs and traffic lights regulate the traffic; they also sometimes make your journey take longer

Explore the way in which such physical barriers are built to protect, but how at the same time they tend to be disruptive. In a similar manner people may build barriers by their behaviour or attitudes to protect themselves from others, and at the same time these barriers disrupt or destroy relationships.

### Activities

- Invite the children to sit in front of a wall, as close as they can get, while they write poems about barriers and the feelings they produce.
- Make a collage of newspaper headlines and articles illustrating human sinfulness; for example, robbery, muggings, killings, etc. Superimpose on the collage prayers like 'Dear God, please forgive.'
- Make crayon rubbings of different surfaces around the church. On each rubbing write a different action that can cause barriers between yourself and other people and yourself and God.

### Projects

- Visit barriers in your local area, including physical barriers and the less concrete ones like traffic lights and 'No entry' signs. Take photographs of the barriers or sketch them. Make a collage of all the barriers you find.
- Produce an illustrated book about barriers. Include a description of how the barriers stop people and separate them from other people or from their objectives.
- Make a model of a medieval castle and fortress, showing how walls, ramparts, moats and dykes were used as barriers to keep different groups of people apart.

### Discussion starters

- Barriers built to protect, like medieval castles and fortresses
- Barriers people build by their behaviour or attitudes
- Barriers we build to keep God out
- God's desire to break down barriers

## Dance/drama

Role play is a good way in which to work out the significance of situations which involve moral choices. Help small groups of children to develop a scene such as the following:

- Rebecca and Siân want to read the same book, and there is a quarrel
- Jeremy eats all the cake and there is none left for the others
- Mother is ill in bed, the children make a noise, and father is angry
- John makes fun of Jeremy, and there is a fight
- No one remembers Ann's birthday, and she is very upset
- Natalie refuses to help set the table for dinner when mother is very busy
- Daniel spills paint on a library book, and puts the blame onto Bethan

## CELEBRATING TOGETHER

### All-age involvement

Invite all members of the congregation to look through local and national papers and magazines for headlines and photographs which illustrate barriers and sinfulness. Display these around the church. Allow time for adults and children to walk round, discussing the display.

### The service

Immediately before the Confession, invite the congregation to reflect on the meaning of sin as a barrier. Draw attention to the activity work on barriers and the collage of newspaper headlines, illustrating the barriers we build against God. If the children have prepared role plays on moral issues, some of these can be presented here. Read Jesus' summary of the law as a preparation for Confession.

### Display

The Confession invites us to examine the barriers we build between ourselves and other people and between ourselves and God. We are sorry about these barriers and ask God to forgive us.

# 4
# The mender

## KEY AIMS

- To help children and adults forgive others
- To help the children explore the range of people whose job it is to mend and to restore
- To help the children understand the priest as pronouncing forgiveness or restored relationships with God
- To help the children appreciate the experience of forgiveness

## WORSHIP RESOURCES

### Reference to communion service

*Absolution*

The Absolution proclaims the forgiveness of sins. It says that the break in the relationship between us and God is mended. To pronounce the forgiveness of sins is one of the sacramental privileges and responsibilities given to the priest in ordination.

### Picture

The picture shows the priest pronouncing God's words of forgiveness and asserting restored relationships with God. As the words of forgiveness are being said, the priest's right hand makes the sign of the cross.

### Bible story

*Forgiveness of sins* (John 20:19-23)

On the first Easter Sunday evening, before they understood Jesus' resurrection, the disciples had met together and locked the door because they were afraid. Then Jesus came and stood there with them. 'Peace be with you!' he said. When the disciples saw the Lord they were filled with joy. Then Jesus commissioned them to carry on with his work. 'As the Father sent me,' he said, 'so I send you.' He breathed on them, saying, 'Receive the Holy Spirit! If you forgive anyone's sins, they are forgiven; if you pronounce them unforgiven, unforgiven they remain.' This passage from St John's Gospel is read when priests are ordained and the bishop passes on to them the authority to absolve sins in Christ's name. That is why the priest gives the Absolution in the communion service and how we can be confident that our sins are forgiven.

## Hymns and songs

*Come and Praise*　　　　　EH
Morning has broken (1)　237
Now the green blade rises (131)　115
Praise to the Lord, the Almighty, the King of creation (34) 440

*Hymns Ancient and Modern New Standard*
Awake, awake: fling off the night! (342)
Now thank we all our God (205) 413
Thine be the glory, risen, conquering Son (428) 120

*Hymns Old and New: New Anglican Edition*
Amazing grace! How sweet the sound (27)
God forgave my sin in Jesus' name (167)
I am a new creation (221)

*Complete Anglican Hymns Old and New*
I'm accepted, I'm forgiven (830)
Jesus is special, special to me (848)
Praise God who forgives all our sins (11)

*Hymns and Songs for Assembly*
God forgave my sin in Jesus' name (33)
I'm accepted, I'm forgiven (52)
The Spirit lives to set us free (112) ✓

## Bible readings

Old Testament – Psalm 32:1-5
New Testament – 1 John 1:8-2:2
*Gospel – John 20:19-23

## Prayer

Forgiving God,
you give to your people
the freedom and joy of your forgiveness.
Help us freely to forgive others
as we have been freely forgiven;
through Jesus Christ our Lord.

## CHILDREN'S WORKSHOP

### Ice-breaker

Bring some pictures of garage breakdown and repair vehicles and the people who operate them. Encourage the children to describe any experience they have had of needing help from these people. How do we recognise the breakdown vehicles and the authorised mechanics? Make a list of other things that need mending and the people who are able to mend them – for example, the shoemaker, the watchmaker, the builder, the heating engineer, the plumber, the telephone engineer, the roadmender, etc. Talk about the people who regularly 'service' mechanical things and why they need regular servicing – for example, the garage mechanic who services the vicar's car, the heating engineer who services the church's

heating system. Develop the idea of the vicar as the one who is authorised to pronounce the restored relationship with God.

### Activities
- Make a display of broken things that need mending. Discuss who would be most suitable for mending each of them. If there are any that you can mend together, do so.
- Make a collage about the shoemaker repairing old shoes. Draw pictures of the shoes, before and after. Show the equipment needed for the repairs and the look of concentration on the shoemaker's face during the mending.
- Make a cartoon sequence of pictures about the car breakdown. Show the arrival of the breakdown vehicle and the car in process of being repaired.

### Projects
- Visit a local garage and talk with a mechanic who is mending a car, or visit a local builder on site at a repair job. Draw before-and-after pictures of the work, or write a report on the worker and how he or she feels about the work of repairing broken articles.
- Make a sequence of murals about various menders at work, for example:
  - the parent repairing a toy car or a doll
  - the shoemaker repairing worn shoes
  - the watchmaker repairing a clock
  - the mechanic and breakdown vehicle repairing a car
  - the builder repairing the church roof
  - the plumber repairing a burst pipe in winter
  - the telephone engineer repairing overhead cables brought down in a storm
  - the roadman repairing a road – using pneumatic drills and road rollers
- Read a parable about forgiveness, such as Matthew 18:21-35, and produce a play about it.

### Discussion starters
- The local repair shops
- The local garage
- The children's experience of having things repaired
- The vicar's authority to pronounce forgiveness of sins

### Dance/drama
Develop a play about the day the car broke down and the way the mechanic came to the rescue. Alternatively, plan some simple dance movements to symbolise restored relationships. Help the children to explore appropriate movements with a partner. Begin with body positions and facial expressions that show anger or rejection. Next explore positions and expressions that show relationships being mended, perhaps with a smile or the word 'sorry' or a handshake. Work out ways to get from one to the other, perhaps with children circling around each other, or facing away and gradually turning back.

# CELEBRATING TOGETHER

## All-age involvement

Invite members of the congregation to bring along articles that they connect with forgiveness – for example, personal objects, photographs, newspaper articles. Display these without asking for personal explanations. Provide a variety of coloured ribbons or streamers. Ask people to think about their feelings after being forgiven, to select a ribbon/streamer in a colour they associate with one of these feelings, and to place it around the display, discussing their choice of colours with others.

## The service

Immediately before the Confession, invite the congregation to reflect on the Absolution as mending our broken relationship with God. Draw attention to the activity work on the mender and to the priest as the one authorised to pronounce God's forgiveness. If the children have developed a play about the car breaking down and being mended, or a dance about relationships, this can be presented before the Confession.

## Display

The Absolution proclaims the forgiveness of sins. It says that the break in the relationship between us and God is mended.

# 5

# Making music

### KEY AIMS

- To help children and adults explore the ancient hymn 'Glory to God'
- To help the children experience the joy of praising God
- To help the children see the relationship between music and praise
- To give the children the opportunity to help lead the congregation's praise

### WORSHIP RESOURCES

#### Reference to communion service

*Glory to God*

The 'Glory to God' is one of the earliest Christian hymns outside the Bible. The opening words echo the song of the angels heard by the shepherds at Bethlehem on the first Christmas. At this early stage in the service the 'Glory to God' prepares us for the fact that the word 'eucharist' itself means 'to give thanks'. As a shout of thanks and praise the 'Glory to God' sets the mood for what follows.

#### Picture

The picture shows children enjoying making music for the praise of God. Their instruments include drum, cymbals, and saxophone. There is a sense of joy in the air.

#### Bible story

*Praising God with the sound of music* (Psalm 150)

Copy out Psalm 150 on to a wall chart or OHP slide for group reading. Practise this, making full use of the speech rhythms:

Praise the Lord.
O praise God in his sanctuary:
praise him in the firmament of his power.

Praise him for his mighty acts:
praise him according to his abundant goodness.

Praise him in the blast of the ram's horn:
praise him upon the lute and harp.

Praise him with the timbrel and dances:
praise him upon the strings and pipe.

Praise him on the high sounding cymbals:
praise him on the loud cymbals.

Let everything that has breath praise the Lord:
O praise the Lord.

(From the Good News Bible)

## Hymns and songs

*Come and Praise*
By brother sun who brings the day (78)
Praise the Lord in the rhythm of your music (33)
There is singing in the desert (26)

*Hymns Ancient and Modern New Standard*
Christ is the world's light, he and none other (440)
'Glory to God!' all heav'n with joy is ringing (462)
O praise ye the Lord! (203)

*Hymns Old and New: New Anglican Edition*
Angel-voices ever singing (33)
New songs of celebration render (350)
Sing to God new songs of worship (447)

*Complete Anglican Hymns Old and New*
Father, we want to thank you (798)
Praise God in his holy place (879)
There was one, there were two (895)

*Hymns and Songs for Assembly*
My God is so big (82)
Praise him on the trumpet (93)
Travel on, travel on, there's a river that is flowing (119)

## Bible readings

*Old Testament – Psalm 150:1-6
New Testament – Ephesians 5:19-20
Gospel – Luke 2:8-14

## Prayer

Lord God,
you give us an ear for music
and a heart for song.
Help us to praise you
with tambourines and dancing,
with recorders and singing,
with the clash of cymbals and the fanfare of trumpets;
through Jesus Christ who lives in harmony
with you and the Holy Spirit,
now and for ever.

## CHILDREN'S WORKSHOP

### Ice-breaker

Make a recording of different musical sounds with which the children are familiar – for example, recorder, tambourine, chime bars, triangle, trumpet, piano, organ. Play these sounds one by one and ask the children to identify them. Choose short extracts of different styles of music and ask the children to express the mood of the music in their movements around the room – for example, slow and sad music, followed by fast and happy music. Ask them to describe the sort of music which best expresses praise and thanksgiving, or to use percussion instruments to create music that expresses praise and thanksgiving.

### Activities

* Write poems based on Psalm 150. Encourage the children to think of modern instruments to include and to use the name of your church or neighbourhood in their poems to make it specific.

* Choose a favourite song or hymn and practise singing it with each child using a musical instrument to accompany the singing.

* Make a mural of different sorts of musical groups, including the pop group seen on television, the church choir, the school orchestra, etc. This can include magazine pictures, photographs and hand-drawn pictures.

### Projects

* Make your own musical instruments. Drums can be made from tins or boxes, which can be decorated with paper collage. Shakers can be made from tins or plastic bottles filled with different objects (for example, pebbles, sand, dried peas, cotton wool) to produce different sounds. A large stringed instrument can be made from a tea chest and broom handle with thick string to twang. A rasping sound is made by rubbing together blocks of wood covered with sandpaper. Rhythm sticks can be made from pieces of dowelling or the handles of wooden spoons.

* Prepare a book about those who praise God with music. Interview the organist, members of the church choir, the conductor (from your own church and from other local churches). Arrange for someone who writes music to come and talk briefly about his or her ideas. Write down the main points from these interviews, using a separate page for each person. You could include photographs. You could record a cassette to go with the book, with samples of music from each person interviewed.

* Learn more about the organ, the instrument usually used in church music. Look at an organ and listen to the richness of its sounds. (Arrange for the organist to play something special like J. S. Bach's 'D Minor Toccata'.) Find out how the sound is varied. Make a model organ case with cardboard tubes for the pipes.

## Discussion starters

- What instruments do the children play, and what would they like to play?
- Invite the children who play instruments to talk about them and demonstrate them
- What instruments do their friends and family play?
- What instruments have they heard others play?

## Dance/drama

Invite the children to listen to J. S. Bach's 'D Minor Toccata', on CD or played on the church organ. Talk about the shapes and colours which the music suggests. If there is time invite the children to paint their feelings in response to the music. Then encourage them to explore in dance the different moods of the Toccata, including its climaxes and its dying away movements. Offer the dance as a hymn of praise to God.

## CELEBRATING TOGETHER

### All-age involvement

Invite all members of the congregation to bring one of their favourite pieces of music to the service, on record, cassette, CD or score, and to mark their name clearly on it. Make space in the service for buzz groups to talk about their choice and then arrange for different types of music to be displayed in different parts of the church – for example, vocal, orchestral, organ, etc., or according to style.

### The service

Before the 'Glory to God' remind the congregation how this great hymn of praise has its roots in the angels' song at Bethlehem, and how song and music play a central part in proclaiming God's praises. Draw attention to the activity work on musical instruments. If the children have prepared movement on the D Minor Toccata this can be presented before the 'Glory to God'. If the children have prepared Psalm 150 as choral speech, this can be presented as the first lesson. If the children have made percussion instruments these can be used to accompany some of the hymns.

### Display

The 'Glory to God' is a great Christian hymn of praise. It has its roots in the angels' song at Bethlehem. Music helps us to express the joy and happiness of our praise.

# 6

# Your clergy

## KEY AIMS

- To help children and adults explore the Collect, the theme prayer offered by the presiding cleric on behalf of the congregation
- To help the children get to know their clergy
- To help the children appreciate the significance of the eucharistic vestments
- To help the children explore the calling of deacons and priests

## WORSHIP RESOURCES

### Reference to communion service

*Collect*

The Collect comes at the beginning of the Ministry of the Word and before the readings from Scripture. There is a special Collect for every Sunday of the Church's year, for the holy days and festivals of the Church, and for the other occasions for which a special set of readings has also been chosen. Generally the Collect sums up the theme of the readings in a short and direct prayer. Since the Collect is one of the early points in the service when the president acts on behalf of the worshipping community, this is a good opportunity to consider the role and function of the clergy.

### Picture

The picture shows the priest leading the Collect on behalf of the people. The priest is wearing a green stole. Different colours are used at different times of the Church's year. Green is used on ordinary Sundays when there are no special festivals or seasons.

### Ordination service

In place of a Scripture passage, study what happens at an ordination service, through the eyes of those who are to be ordained. They have been away to a 'selection conference', where they have been carefully interviewed and their suitability assessed. They have been selected for training. They have been on a training course, to study, to acquire professional skills and to grow in prayer. The ordination service probably takes place in the cathedral. Now read through the ordination service in the modern prayer book.

## Hymns and songs

*Come and Praise*
Give me oil in my lamp, keep me burning (43)
If I had a hammer (71)
It's the springs up in the mountains (82)

*Hymns Ancient and Modern New Standard*
Dear Lord, to you again our gifts we bring (352)
Disposer supreme, and Judge of the earth (298)
Fill thou my life, O Lord my God (200)

*Hymns Old and New: New Anglican Edition*
Come down, O love divine (90)
Thy way, not mine, O Lord (521)
We have a gospel to proclaim (532)

*Complete Anglican Hymns Old and New*
Come, Holy Ghost, our souls inspire (118)
Take me, Lord, use my life (623)
Ye servants of the Lord (757)

*Hymns and Songs for Assembly*
God's Spirit is in my heart (36)
I give my hands to do your work (48)
The bell of creation (107)

## Bible readings

*Old Testament – Malachi 2:5-7
New Testament – 1 Timothy 3:8-13
Gospel – John 20:19-23

## Prayer

Almighty God,
you call deacons and priests
to your service.
Strengthen those whom you have called
that they may faithfully serve you,
to the glory of your name
and to the benefit of your Church;
through Jesus Christ, our great High Priest.

## CHILDREN'S WORKSHOP

### Ice-breaker
Invite the clergy to show to the children the stoles and other vestments
worn for the eucharist. If the church possesses different coloured sets
of vestments, display them on tables so that the children can see that
each set contains the same items. Talk about the reason for the different
colours:

- white for festivals like Christmas and Easter and Saints days

- purple for the penitential seasons like Advent and Lent

- red for the Holy Spirit at Whitsun and for martyrs
- green for the ordinary days

Then ask the clergy to show the children how to vest. The children may also like to try the vestments on themselves.

### Activities

- Try to discover the names of the clergy who have served your local church since it was built. Try to discover pictures or photographs of some of the former clergy. See if there are memorials inside the church or gravestones outside commemorating the former clergy. Make rubbings of these memorials. Some churches may have ancient memorial brasses of priests which make excellent brass rubbings.

- Interview your clergy about how they spend a working day and how they spend their day off. Find out about them as people as well as clergy. What are their favourite foods and what do they like for breakfast? What are their everyday tasks connected with the church?

- Read some collects in order to understand the style, then write your own.

### Projects

- For a longer term project, after interviewing your clergy you could invite the children to imagine that they are ordained and to write or draw about 'a day in my life as a deacon or priest'. Children could work together, each choosing a different incident.

- On a large sheet of paper draw round a child and then draw in the outline of the vestments, including a simple pattern on the chasuble. Different groups of children can produce paper vestments in the four liturgical colours, or they could make and decorate a real set of vestments to be used by the priest or modelled by the children.

- Prepare and present your own 'This is Your Life' about the life story of a typical priest. The children can pretend to be parents, school friends, college friends, wife or husband, children, parishioners, etc. Develop questions that show the priest to be an ordinary person with a special role.

### Discussion starters

- How many deacons and priests do the children know?
- What do deacons and priests do?
- Do deacons and priests always have to wear special clothing?
- How do people become deacons and priests?

### Dance/drama

Develop a short series of tableaux, mimes or acts about a day in the life of the parish clergy, illustrating some of the things they do and some of the people they meet.

# CELEBRATING TOGETHER

## All-age involvement

Make available paper and pens and ask people to draw or write about one function of the clergy that has been important to them at some time in their lives. These could be gathered together and held during a special prayer of thanks for the work of the clergy within the church.

## The service

When the Collect for the day has been prayed, draw the congregation's attention to the fact that this prayer has been offered on their behalf and invite them to think about the role of the clergy in the life of their church. Draw attention to the activity work and invite the children to display the vestments they have made. If they have prepared drama on the life of the priest this can be presented here.

## Display

When the president says the Collect, this prayer is offered on behalf of the whole congregation. The Collect makes us think of the clergy's special function in the church.

# 7

# Hear all about it

## KEY AIMS

- To help children and adults explore how the Bible is used in the communion service
- To help the children recognise the Bible as a library of books
- To help the children appreciate that the Bible contains different kinds of literature
- To help the children grasp that God still speaks to us today through the Bible

## WORSHIP RESOURCES

### Reference to communion service

*Ministry of the Word*

The readings from Scripture play a central part in the Church's worship. The lectionary appoints three readings for every Sunday and for other key days in the Church's year, one reading each from the Old Testament, the New Testament and the Gospels. The readings are usually integrated around a common theme. The responses after the readings ('This is the word of the Lord' and 'This is the Gospel of the Lord') are in the present tense to indicate that God speaks today through the reading of the word. The sermon provides an opportunity to comment on and to interpret the readings.

### Picture

The picture shows a child reading and enjoying a wide range of different books. This helps to remind us that the Bible contains a variety of different books.

### Bible story

*Jesus reads from the Bible in Nazareth* (Luke 4:1-21)

Jesus used to go to the synagogue on the Sabbath day. Sometimes he was asked to read from the Bible and to interpret the reading in an address. In those days the Bible was not printed like the books we know today. Printing had not been invented. Instead the Bibles were written out by hand on long scrolls. One day when Jesus was visiting his home town of Nazareth they asked him to read the lesson and handed him the scroll of the prophet Isaiah. He opened the scroll and read the passage which says, 'The Spirit of the Lord is upon me because he has anointed me.' Then he rolled up the scroll, gave it back to the attendant and sat down to teach. 'Today,' he said, 'in your very hearing this text has come true.' In the same way every Sunday we listen to the words of the Bible read in church and the preacher helps us to understand what those words mean for us today. 'This is the word of the Lord: thanks be to God.'

## Hymns and songs

*Come and Praise*
Ev'ry word comes alive (72)
Go, tell it on the mountain (24)
Rejoice in the Lord always (95)

*Hymns Ancient and Modern New Standard*
Lord, I have made thy word my choice (490)
Lord Jesus, once you spoke to men (392)
Lord, thy word abideth (166)

*Hymns Old and New: New Anglican Edition*
I will sing the wondrous story (237)
Now, my tongue, the myst'ry telling (353)
One shall tell another (406)

*Complete Anglican Hymns Old and New*
Go, tell it on the mountain (243)
Jesus had all kinds of friends (846)
There is so much to discover (891)

*Hymns and Songs for Assembly*
How lovely on the mountains are the feet (45)
I planted a seed (58)
Seek ye first the kingdom of God (99)

## Bible readings

Old Testament – Nehemiah 8:5-8
New Testament – 2 Timothy 3:14-17
*Gospel – Luke 4:14-21

## Prayer

Blessed Lord,
you have given the Bible to your people.
Help us to hear your word,
that we may know you clearly,
love you deeply
and serve you fully;
through Jesus Christ, your living Word.

## CHILDREN'S WORKSHOP

### Ice-breaker

Arrange for the children to visit a public library or a school library (or, if this is not possible, to look at pictures of libraries). Talk about all the different kinds of books. Note how they are organised on the shelf or in the display racks, by subjects, size or reading difficulty. Note how the books differ in their sizes, shapes, number of pages, print designs, covers, and so on. Then look at the Bible and see how that is made up as a library of books. Note the difference between the Old Testament and the New Testament. Discover where the Gospels come and how many Gospels there are. Explore the different lengths, styles and contents of the books of the Bible.

### Activities

- Make scrolls from long lengths of paper, fastened to a cardboard tube as a handle. Decorate the handles. Some children may like to write a scroll for themselves, either as creative writing or copying a passage from the Bible.

- Show a film or slides on the history of the Bible.

- Write 'eye-witness' accounts of Jesus' visit to the synagogue in Nazareth (Luke 4:14-21).

### Projects

- Write a Bible newspaper. The Bible is rather like a newspaper; it contains a lot of material of different kinds – for example, history, poetry, law, wisdom, riddles, stories, letters. Encourage the children to write about and illustrate their favourite Bible stories in a way suitable for newsprint, choosing cartoons, advertisements, headlines, or whatever is most appropriate for their chosen stories – for example, the stars foretelling the coming of the wise men, the weather column foretelling seven years of drought (Joseph), or the travel column describing the Exodus (Moses).

- Make a Bible library. Each book of the Bible can be represented as a different volume. Empty cardboard packets or old books can be covered with different sorts of 'binding' and the names of the books of the Bible inscribed on the spines. Different coloured bindings can be used to distinguish Old Testament books from New Testament books, or the different kinds of book in each testament. Different sizes can be used for different lengths of books. When made the books can be put in various groups – for example, the order they appear in The New English Bible or The Jerusalem Bible or according to the type of material they contain.

- Look at Hebrew, Greek and Latin Bibles, and pictures of illuminated manuscripts. The children can copy these forms of writing, or write their own name or the name of a book of the Bible in illuminated script.

### Discussion starters
- Which books have the children read recently?
- What kind of books do the children most like reading?
- What are the names of the books of the Bible and what do these names tell us about their contents?
- What are the different kinds of books in the Bible?

### Dance/drama
Let the children use the lectern and pulpit in church to practise reading the Scriptures aloud. Try different ways of reading, using choral speech or dramatic parts. Record the children's voices.

## CELEBRATING TOGETHER

### All-age involvement
Invite members of the congregation to bring along their own Bibles and to display these, open at a passage that holds meaning for them. Invite a few people, children and adults, to read aloud a single verse, each verse to be chosen from a different book of the Bible to show different kinds of literature. Finish with the affirmation, 'This is the word of the Lord: thanks be to God.'

### The service
After the Collect invite the congregation to think about what they are affirming when they say after the readings, 'This is the word of the Lord' or 'This is the Gospel of the Lord.' Draw attention to the activity work on the Bible. Encourage the children to take a key role in the Ministry of the Word by reading the lessons; let the readers make a ceremony of handing over and receiving the Bible.

### Display
The Bible is a rich library of books, including history, poetry, prophecy, letters, gospels. In the Ministry of the Word, God speaks afresh to people today through the Bible.

# 8

# Follow the signs

## KEY AIMS

- To help children and adults explore the first part of the Creed, 'We believe in God'
- To help the children explore the ways signs and symbols work
- To help the children explore key images used to speak of God
- To help the children appreciate both the fun and difficulty involved in talking about God

## WORSHIP RESOURCES

### Reference to communion service

*We believe in God*

Our ideas and language about God are built up by a number of images. No one image is sufficient in itself. We need to see what each image has to say and then pass on to the next image. The problem with images is that they easily become mistaken for the reality to which they point. The danger is that when we begin by saying God is like a father, we conclude by being content with the idea that God is an old man in the sky. Our images of God are never the final truth: they are signs and symbols which point beyond themselves.

### Picture

The picture represents the presence of God in the world through a bright flame. This reminds us of the way in which Moses came to recognise the presence of God through the flame in the burning bush. The flame is but one powerful image or symbol for God the Father.

### Bible story

*The burning bush* (Exodus 3:1-6)

Moses was out in the wilderness, looking after the sheep of his father-in-law, Jethro. God had chosen Moses for the special task of leading his people to a new country. While he was minding the sheep, Moses saw a burning bush. Although the bush was on fire, it was not being burnt up. When Moses turned aside to look at the bush, God spoke to him out of the bush and called him by name, 'Moses, Moses.' And Moses answered, 'Yes, I am here.' It was through the burning bush that Moses came to hear the voice of God.

## Hymns and songs

*Come and Praise*
A still small voice in the heart of the city (96)
God who made the earth (10)
Who put the colours in the rainbow? (12)

*Hymns Ancient and Modern New Standard*
All my hope on God is founded (336)
Immortal, invisible, God only wise (199)
With wonder, Lord, we see your works (531)

*Hymns Old and New: New Anglican Edition*
Father God, I wonder (119)
Immortal, invisible, God only wise (242)
O God of earth and altar (365)

*Complete Anglican Hymns Old and New*
God is love (215)
God is our strength and refuge (219)
God is working his purpose out (221)

*Hymns and Songs for Assembly*
God is love: his the care (34)
Think big: an elephant (114)
When your Father made the world (129)

## Bible readings

*Old Testament – Exodus 3:1-6
New Testament – Romans 8:14-17
Gospel – Luke 11:1-4

## Prayer

Dear Lord God,
you are a mighty rock,
protect us.
You are a shepherd,
care for us.
You are a vinedresser,
shape us.
You are a king,
rule over us.
You are a guardian,
love us.
You are a still small voice,
speak to us.
We make our prayer
in the name of Jesus Christ our Lord.

## CHILDREN'S WORKSHOP

### Ice-breaker

Copy a number of traffic signs onto posters or OHP slides and hold a quiz to see how many the children recognise. Draw attention to the clues they pick up from the colours and shapes of traffic signs. Draw attention to the way signs point beyond themselves to something bigger: at a crossroads a decision has to be taken about the direction in which to go; when danger is signposted care has to be taken. Then encourage the children to talk about some signs and images used to speak of God – for example, father, king, shepherd, vinedresser, rock, fire, small voice. Explore what these signs are saying about God.

### Activities

- Make a display of trademarks on foodstuffs. You will need to bring to the group a selection of food products from which they can choose.
- Look for signs and symbols in the local church. Each child could copy a different symbol. Discuss how these add to our understanding of God. Think of modern, everyday images that could give us new pictures of God – for example, the 'lollipop lady' making the road safe for us.
- Draw a set of pictures of road signs.

### Projects

- Make life-size models of road signs using white paper and black paint for pedestrian crossings, balloons and large cardboard tubes as traffic lights, etc.
- Produce posters illustrating some of the images we use to speak of God – for example, shepherd, father, king, vinedresser, rock, fire.
- Make a set of playing cards to play 'Highway Code Snap' or 'Symbol Snap'. Choose at least eight signs or symbols and draw four cards for each symbol. Take care that each card is the same size. Play the game according to the usual 'Snap' rules.

### Discussion starters

- Signs used as trademarks – for example, brand names for foods
- Signs used on shops – for example, McDonald's
- Signs used on cars – for example, the Rolls-Royce radiator grille
- International picture signs – for example, public lavatories
- Signs on badges and scarves – for example, football colours

### Dance/drama

Devise a dance to tell the story of Moses and the burning bush – how he approaches the bush with uncertainty and curiosity, how he is overawed when God speaks to him, etc.

# CELEBRATING TOGETHER

## All-age involvement

Point out all the signs and symbols that are in your church building to teach about different aspects of God. Ask the congregation to move and stand next to the symbol that is most familiar to them, thinking about what they know of God from that image. Then ask them to stand next to the symbol they have thought least about in the past, allowing a few moments for quiet reflection on what they can learn about God from that image.

## The service

Before the Creed encourage the congregation to think about the difficulty we have in finding the right words to talk about God. Draw their attention to the activity work on road signs and to the range of images they have explored to talk about God. The children's road signs can be used to hold a quiz among the congregation, to see how well they know the Highway Code.

## Display

We use signs and images to talk about God. God is like a parent who loves us, a shepherd who cares for us, a vinedresser who shapes us, a rock who protects us.

# 9

# Meeting Jesus of Nazareth

## KEY AIMS

- To help children and adults explore the second part of the Creed, 'We believe in Jesus Christ'
- To help the children place Jesus in time and history
- To help the children appreciate some of the gospel accounts of Jesus
- To help the children celebrate their faith in Jesus

## WORSHIP RESOURCES

### Reference to communion service

*We believe in Jesus Christ*

The Church's belief in Jesus Christ contains two essential components. First, it is committed to faith in a person who lived at a specific time and place in history. Second, it is committed to the belief that this person is none other than God incarnate who is worthy of our worship and praise. The Creed stresses that the Jesus whom we worship in the eucharist was made man, was crucified, rose again and ascended into heaven.

### Picture

The picture shows children gazing at the empty cross. The cross is the internationally recognised symbol for Jesus. The cross speaks to us of Jesus' death by crucifixion; the empty cross speaks also of his glorious resurrection from the dead.

### Bible story

In place of a shared reading from Scripture, invite the children to divide into small groups. Ask each group to take one main event from the life of Jesus, to talk about that event among themselves and with the teacher, and then to make a big poster illustrating the event. While they are working talk with the groups about their ideas and the themes they have chosen. Try to make sure that posters are produced about the birth, the cross and the empty tomb. Other posters will emerge on themes which are important to the children. Ideas might include the call of the first

disciples (Mark 1:16-18), Jesus the healer (Mark 1:40-41), Jesus the teacher (Mark 4:1-2), Jesus feeds the five thousand (Mark 6:35-44). When the posters are complete, prepare a caption for each and arrange their display in church.

## Hymns and songs
*Come and Praise*
I saw the man from Galilee (75)
There is singing in the desert (26)
There's a child in the streets (27)

*Hymns Ancient and Modern New Standard*
A Man there lived in Galilee (334)
I danced in the morning (375)
When morning gilds the skies (146)

*Hymns Old and New: New Anglican Edition*
All hail the pow'r of Jesus' name (13)
Angels from the realms of glory (34)
At the name of Jesus (46)

*Complete Anglican Hymns Old and New*
All of the people on the mountain (772)
Jesus is Lord (352)
Put your trust in the man (882)

*Hymns and Songs for Assembly*
Come and praise the Lord our King (19)
When Jesus walked in Galilee (128)
Who is king of the jungle (131)

## Bible readings
Old Testament – Isaiah 9:6-7
New Testament – Acts 1:9-11
*Gospel – Luke 24:1-9

## Prayer
God our guide,
you led the shepherds to see the infant Jesus;
you led the disciples to see the risen Lord.
Lead us to know his presence with us,
that we may share his risen life.
He lives and reigns
with you and the Holy Spirit,
now and always.

## CHILDREN'S WORKSHOP

### Ice-breaker
Borrow pictures, slides, film strips or videos from a local resource centre which show Palestine today or during the time of Jesus. Alternatively, if members of the local church have been to the Holy Land, invite them to

talk for five minutes about their visit and to display the pictures and artefacts they brought back. Draw out the children's ideas of the ways Palestine is different from their own country and how things were different 2000 years ago.

### Activities

- Make a collection of Christmas cards which portray Jesus, Mary, Joseph, the shepherds, the kings. Note the huge variety of images and how they have changed through the ages.
- Draw a map of Palestine and note some of the places Jesus knew. You could do this as a group activity on a large map or someone could photocopy outlines in advance for each person. Look at a large map to draw in place names. You may also like to add symbols for some of the stories – for example, a star by Bethlehem, five loaves and two fish at Bethsaida, Zacchaeus' tree at Jericho, a cross at Jerusalem.
- Imagine you are one of Jesus' closest friends (Peter or Mary Magdalene) and write about Jesus as you knew him.

### Projects

- Plan a radio or television interview with Jesus' friends. Write the scripts in pairs, an interviewer plus Jesus' friend. You could tape them on either audio cassette or video.
- Create a model of a Palestinian village, such as Nazareth. Include houses with flat roofs and outside steps; a carpenter's shop with bench, tools, etc.; the market place with corn, olive oil, sheep, goats, etc.; the well with women carrying water in pitchers; small figures made of pegs or pipe cleaners dressed in Palestinian clothes to be story tellers, traders, shepherds, farmers, wine makers, wedding guests, etc.
- Create a frieze on the life of Jesus to cover the walls of a whole room or corridor. Use Bible passages from the Gospel of Luke (see Bible story) as the basis. Each passage could be represented by a different picture.

### Discussion starters

- Make a list of all the things we have which Jesus did not have in first-century Palestine
- Look at pictures of Jesus in the local church, such as stained glass windows, and compare these with pictures the children have seen in other churches or in art galleries and museums
- What do the children know about the life of Jesus?
- Ask about the four Gospel writers who give us our information about Jesus

### Dance/drama

Devise a dance to tell the major points in the life of Jesus: his birth, the years of ministry, his death and resurrection. Perhaps the dance could start with one person cradling a baby then going off stage. The adult Jesus could appear and 'call' followers, and so on.

# CELEBRATING TOGETHER

## All-age involvement

Ask each member of the congregation to remember their favourite story of Jesus and to think of a few words to summarise this. Hand out coloured streamers and felt pens. These messages about Jesus can be written on the streamers, and the streamers can be used to decorate the pews.

## The service

Before the Creed draw the congregation's attention to the activity work on Jesus Christ. Display the models of Nazareth and the collection of Christmas cards. If the children have prepared a dance on the life of Jesus, this can be presented between the second and third parts of the Creed to interpret what has just been said.

## Display

Jesus was born in Palestine about 2000 years ago. He was crucified and rose from the dead. We believe Jesus is the Son of God.

# 10

# Windy day

### KEY AIMS

- To help children and adults explore the third section of the Creed, 'We believe in the Holy Spirit'
- To help the children experience and think about the mystery of the wind
- To help the children study the effects of the wind on simple things like sailing boats, kites and windmills
- To help the children see the link between the wind and God the Holy Spirit

### WORSHIP RESOURCES

#### Reference to communion service

*We believe in the Holy Spirit*

The key image used to speak about God the Holy Spirit is the wind. The image of the wind and the reality of God the Holy Spirit are so closely associated that the same word is used for 'wind' and for 'spirit' in both Hebrew (ruach) and Greek (pneuma). Like the wind, God the Holy Spirit is all around us. We cannot see the Holy Spirit and yet we experience the Spirit's effect on us.

#### Picture

The picture shows children out on a windy day, flying kites. The picture reminds us how the wind is a powerful image for God the Holy Spirit.

#### Bible story

*Day of Pentecost* (Acts 2:1-4)

After Jesus rose from the dead on Easter Sunday he appeared to his disciples and taught them about the kingdom of God over a period of 40 days. He promised them that he would send the Holy Spirit to them. On the day of Pentecost all the disciples were together in the same place. Suddenly there came from the sky a noise like a strong driving wind which filled the whole house where they were sitting. And there appeared to them tongues like flames of fire, which rested on each of them. And they were all filled with the Holy Spirit. The Holy Spirit gave them new power to proclaim the good news about Jesus and the resurrection.

## Hymns and songs

*Come and Praise*
All creatures of our God and King (7)
Spirit of God, as strong as the wind (63)
Spirit of peace, come to our waiting world (85)

*Hymns Ancient and Modern New Standard*
Christians, lift up your hearts (444)
Gracious Spirit, Holy Ghost (154)
Let every Christian pray (478)

*Hymns Old and New: New Anglican Edition*
Come, Holy Ghost, our hearts inspire (91)
O Breath of Life (356)
O Holy Spirit, Lord of grace (371)

*Complete Anglican Hymns Old and New*
Breathe on me, Breath of God (84)
Holy Spirit, truth divine (289)
You've got to move (918)

*Hymns and Songs for Assembly*
All over the world the Spirit is moving (4)
Spirit of God (102)
Spirit of peace (103)

## Bible readings

Old Testament – Ezekiel 37:1-10
*New Testament – Acts 2:1-4
Gospel – John 14:15-18

## Prayer

Almighty God,
you sent your Holy Spirit
like the wind from heaven,
to strengthen the disciples.
Fill us with the same Spirit
that we may share in their work;
through Jesus Christ our Lord.

## CHILDREN'S WORKSHOP

### Ice-breaker

Arrange for the children to experience some signs of the power of the wind. Either take them outside to fly a kite, or stay indoors and give them each a balloon to blow up. Talk about what the wind is like and what it does. You cannot see the wind, yet you can see it blow washing on the line. You cannot touch the wind, yet you can feel it blow against you. You cannot hear the wind, yet you can hear it shake the trees and dustbin lids.

## Activities

- Write a poem about a windy day, recording it with sound effects.
- Paper darts and aeroplanes can be made in a number of different ways from folding paper. Many children already know their own way of making these things. Encourage them to compare their different methods and different models, and to experiment with their flight patterns.
- Make small hand-held windmills. From each corner of a piece of paper, cut in towards the centre. Take the four corners to the centre and push a pin through these into a straw.

## Projects

- Make a large model windmill with flanged edges on the sails for the wind to push against.
- Make kites from wood and paper. The kites can be painted and the string can be decorated with coloured tissue paper bows.
- Small sailing boats which really float can be made simply from a piece of shaped wood. A sail can be made from card or scrap material.

## Discussion starters

- The noise of the wind
- The feeling of being out on a windy day
- The effect of wind on a heap of leaves

## Dance/drama

Devise movement about a windy day. Encourage the children to be trees beaten by the wind, leaves blown by the wind, windmills turned by the wind, kites taken up by the wind, gliders supported by the wind, washing blown about by the wind on the clothes line, a candle being extinguished by the wind, etc.

# CELEBRATING TOGETHER

## All-age involvement

Invite members of the congregation to bring something to church which reminds them of the wind or of some special occasion when wind made an impression on them. Arrange for buzz groups to give the opportunity for individuals to share their object and to tell its story.

## The service

Before the Creed draw the congregation's attention to the activity work on the wind. Display the kites, windmills, aeroplanes, etc. If the children have prepared movement on the theme of a windy day, this can be presented during the third section of the Creed after the phrase 'who has spoken through the prophets', to interpret what has just been said. Blow up a large number of balloons, so that everyone in church can take one home, including the adults. Suspend these balloons in the rafters of the church, so that they can be released at the end of the service and float down among the worshippers.

## Display

The image which tells us most about God the Holy Spirit is the picture of the wind. We cannot see the wind and yet we know that it is there, all around us.

# 11
# Between friends

## KEY AIMS

- To help children and adults explore the invitation to pray for Church and world
- To help the children understand prayer as communication between friends
- To help the children appreciate that everything they do, and everything that makes them happy, sad or afraid is important to God
- To help the children become more aware of the people, situations and issues about which God wishes them to pray

## WORSHIP RESOURCES

### Reference to communion service

*Invitation to prayer*

The prayers of the people include both intercession and thanksgiving. The invitation reminds us that God is concerned with all that takes place in our lives and that he wishes us to share our lives with him. He wants us to talk with him about all that makes us happy or sad. He wants us to share our fears, sorrows, frustrations and joys. God also wishes us to share his concern for his world.

### Picture

The picture shows children busily engaged in a range of activities which they are enjoying: at home with a book, using the computer, and playing in the park. God is interested in the whole of their lives and wants to listen as they give thanks in prayer for their recreation.

### Bible story

*Jesus spends time in prayer* (Mark 1:32-38)

St Mark's Gospel shows that Jesus often lived a very busy and very full life. People crowded around him to hear his teaching and to be healed by him. One evening it seemed as if the whole town was gathered around the house where he was staying. Even after sunset they kept bringing to him all who were ill or possessed by devils. He healed many and drove out many devils. Very early next morning Jesus got up and went out alone. He went away to a lonely spot and stayed there in prayer. These occasions of quiet and prayer were very important to Jesus as times when he could share his life with God the Father. We, too, need time to share with God, to tell God what we have been doing and to listen carefully to what God wants of us.

## Hymns and songs
*Come and Praise*
I will bring to you the best gift I can offer (59)
Sad, puzzled eyes of small hungry children (74)
Think of all the things we lose (57)

*Hymns Ancient and Modern New Standard*
Life is great! So sing about it (482)    EH
Lord, teach us how to pray aright (227)  406
There's a spirit in the air (515)

*Hymns Old and New: New Anglican Edition*
Father, hear the prayer we offer (120)  − 357
O God of Bethel, by whose hand (364)
Thy kingdom come! on bended knee (520)  500

*Complete Anglican Hymns Old and New*
God's love is deeper than the deepest ocean (809)
I have a friend who is deeper than the ocean (829)
Prayer is like a telephone (880)

*Hymns and Songs for Assembly*
Father, I place into your hands (23)
I have a friend who is deeper than the ocean (49)
In the morning early (57)

## Bible readings
Old Testament – Psalm 119:164-168
New Testament – 1 Timothy 2:1-4
*Gospel – Mark 1:32-38

## Prayer
Almighty God,
you take an interest in all we do
and listen to what we have to say.
Help us to hear your word
that we may learn to pray
the prayers you desire from us;
through Jesus Christ our Lord.

## CHILDREN'S WORKSHOP

### Ice-breaker
Invite the children to sit in small groups to share with each other the things that are of interest and of importance to them, or to tell about the things they most enjoyed doing the previous week. If the children sit in

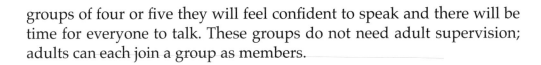

groups of four or five they will feel confident to speak and there will be time for everyone to talk. These groups do not need adult supervision; adults can each join a group as members.

### Activities

- Make an audio tape about the things that are of interest and importance to you, as expressed during the ice-breaker. The groups can take turns in recording material. Perhaps the tape can later be shared with others in the church.

- Make string telephones by joining two cans or plastic cups by a taut length of string. Experiment to see how long a piece of string you can use and still hear each other. Encourage the children to communicate with each other during the week by phone, and with God by prayer.

- Make postboxes from cardboard, painted in the appropriate colour. Encourage the children to use the boxes at home as a reminder, so they communicate with each other by post during the week, especially when one of them is absent. Remind them that they can communicate with God by prayer.

### Projects

- Make a 'prayer board', a notice board divided into the sections of the prayer for the Church and the world, with appropriate headings like *the Church, the world, the local community, the sick, the departed*. Encourage the children to write short prayers to be pinned to the board in the appropriate places. This board can be added to week by week.

- Make a set of posters of the children's favourite activities, to display in church as part of their prayer, telling God about themselves. If there is a special place in the neighbourhood which the children enjoy (a park, a place by the river, an adventure playground), encourage them to talk about it and to produce a poster or model describing it.

- Bring in books about morse code, semaphore, sign language, etc. Let the children experiment and communicate with each other in these ways.

### Discussion starters

- Different modes of communication with friends: talking, telephone, writing letters, etc.

- Things we want to know about our friends when we have not seen them for a while

- What God wants us to pray about

### Dance/drama

Set up a game in which the children have to communicate without speech, where one group acts out an idea and another group has to guess what it is.

# CELEBRATING TOGETHER

## All-age involvement

Invite all members of the congregation to bring to church something to represent what they like doing in their spare time – for example, golf clubs, knitting, cookery book, car maintenance tools. Arrange for buzz groups to explore why these activities appeal and how they can suggest material for prayer. Some individuals may talk briefly about their recreation to the whole congregation and suggest prayer leads flowing from it.

## The service

Before the invitation to pray for the Church and for the world, invite the congregation to reflect on the idea of prayer. Discuss how the children have seen prayer as conversation between friends, telling God what is of interest to them as well as trying to share God's concerns for the world. Draw attention to their posters. If they produced tapes, short extracts can be played. If they have produced a 'prayer board', the congregation can be invited to use it.

## Display

The prayer for the Church and for the world reminds us that we should talk with God about everything that is important to us. At the same time, we should share in God's concerns for the world.

# 12

# Meeting
# the Church

### KEY AIMS

- To help children and adults pray for the Church
- To help the children know their local church better
- To help the children know more about other local churches
- To help the children appreciate the worldwide nature of the Church

### WORSHIP RESOURCES

#### Reference to communion service

*Prayer for the Church*

When we pray for the Church we think of millions of Christian people throughout the world. People of different nationalities, languages and denominations are united through their common membership of Christ's Church. We pray especially for those called by God to lead the worship of the Church and to teach God's people. We pray for bishops, priests, deacons and lay leaders.

#### Picture

The picture shows the clergy and lay people who are the Church of Christ. The bishop is wearing a cope and carrying his pastoral staff. The priest is wearing a white surplice and green stole. The choir boys are wearing red cassocks.

#### Bible story

*Jesus builds his Church* (Matthew 16:13–19)

Jesus' 12 close friends, the disciples, shared his life very closely. They went with him from place to place; they listened to his teaching and shared in his work of healing. After they had been with him for a long time, Jesus challenged them with a question to see if they had really recognised who he was. It was Peter who answered, 'You are the Christ, the Son of the Living God!' Jesus said to Peter, 'You are favoured indeed! You did not learn that from other people. God himself showed you that. You, Peter, are the rock on which I will build my Church.' Now Jesus'

Church has been built throughout the world. Men and women of all races have joined Peter to become the Church of Christ. And you and I are part of that great worldwide Church, built on Peter.

## Hymns and songs

*Come and Praise*                                                    E.H.
At the name of Jesus ev'ry knee shall bow (58)    338
In Christ there is no east or west (66)    480
You've got to move when the spirit says move (107)

*Hymns Ancient and Modern New Standard*
Let the Lord's people, heart and voice uniting (479)
The Church's one foundation (170)    484
Who are we who stand and sing? (529)

*Hymns Old and New: New Anglican edition*
A new commandment (4)
Christ is made the sure foundation (76)    205
City of God, how broad and far (85)    346

*Complete Anglican Hymns Old and New*
I'm black, I'm white, I'm short, I'm tall (832)
The Church of God a kingdom is (635)    483
Wherever you go I will go (744)

*Hymns and Songs for Assembly*
All over the world the Spirit is moving (4)
Bind us together, Lord (15)
Father welcomes all his children (25)

## Bible readings
Old Testament – Numbers 27:15-20
New Testament – 1 Thessalonians 1:1-5
*Gospel – Matthew 16:13-19

## Prayer
Almighty God,
you call people of all races
into membership of your Church.
Hear our prayer for your people,
that all may serve you faithfully
to the glory of your holy name;
through our Lord and Saviour Jesus Christ.

## CHILDREN'S WORKSHOP

### Ice-breaker
Talk about the people who go to the local church. Build up a list of these people: the vicar, curate, readers, organist, choir, churchwardens, PCC members, treasurer, bell-ringers, verger, sacristan, servers, cleaners, flower arrangers, the congregation, the different organisations and committees

like the Mothers' Union, Sunday School, etc. Talk about their different jobs. Invite some of them to talk with the children about what they do; perhaps the bell-ringers will demonstrate their art, the sacristan show them how to prepare for the communion service, the organist display the organ, or the cleaners allow the children to share in their work. Develop the idea of the Church as a family and how the family of the local church shares with the whole Church throughout the world.

### Activities
- Draw a picture of the local church building and draw round it in a circle all the people who contribute to the life of the church, naming them where possible. Include a caption praying for the whole congregation.
- Invite the children to make mitres so that they can pretend to be a group of bishops representing the worldwide Church.
- If your church is an old one, help the children get to know it well. Talk about when it was built and the people who used to worship there. Make rubbings of different surfaces inside and outside the church, and mount them for display. Find out information from the tombstones and memorials. Make a plan of the church, including important features such as the font, pulpit, altar, pews, etc.

### Projects
- Borrow a display figure or cut out a life-size figure from cardboard and dress this to look like a bishop. Make a mitre from cardboard, covered in cloth. Make a pastoral staff from a garden cane covered in tin foil. Make a cope, perhaps using appliqué.
- Visit some of the other local denominations and draw attention to the features which help to characterise these denominations – for example, the baptistry in the Baptist church, the central pulpit in the Free churches, the musical instruments in the Salvation Army citadel, the reserved sacrament in the Catholic church. Make a poster about these visits. Include a caption praying for these churches.
- Help the children to understand how their own church and parish fits into the wider structure of a deanery, an archdeaconry and a diocese. Produce a map of the area showing the parishes of your deanery. Use the diocesan handbooks to find the names of the churches, the clergy and the churchwardens, etc. Add pictures or photographs of the local churches, clergy and the diocesan bishop.

### Discussion starters
- Local churches of different denominations
- The local church's immediate links with the wider Church. Who has met the rural dean, the archdeacon, the bishop?
- What a bishop does
- Ways of praying for the Church

### Dance/drama
Invite the children to prepare a play about the bishop coming to visit their church.

## CELEBRATING TOGETHER

### All-age involvement
Display sheets of paper, each headed with the name of a different church in your area and a picture or photograph of that church. Ask members of the congregation to write in the names of people they know who attend those churches. Pray for the church, naming all the people on your lists.

### The service
After the invitation to prayer, invite the congregation to think especially about their responsibility to pray for the Church, beginning with their own congregation and leaders, the deanery and rural dean, the diocese and the bishops, local churches of other denominations, and then the worldwide Church. Draw attention to the importance of the bishop in symbolising the continuity between the local church and the worldwide Church. Introduce the children's model of the bishop and their work on the local congregation.

### Display
When we pray for the Church, we think of millions of Christian people throughout the world. Our own church is part of that worldwide fellowship.

# 13

# Around the world

### KEY AIMS

- To help children and adults pray for the world
- To help the children know more about God's world and the peoples who live in it
- To help the children respect other races and cultures as God's people
- To help the children be alert to God's care and concern for his world

### WORSHIP RESOURCES

#### Reference to communion service
*Prayer for the world*
When we pray for the world we think of all that God created and every-one for whom Christ died. We need to share in God's care and love for the peoples of the world. We pray especially for our own nation and for all the nations of the world. We pray for all those in authority. We pray for causes of national and international concern.

#### Picture
The picture shows children and young people from across the world. They are sharing together their different foods and customs. This reminds us how people from different backgrounds across the world can build lives together.

#### Bible story
*The many languages of the world* (Genesis 11:1-9 and Acts 2:5-11)
Once upon a time, all the world spoke a single language and used the same words. 'Come,' they said, 'let us build ourselves a city and a tower with its top in the heavens, and make a name for ourselves.' So they made bricks, baked them hard and built tall. God was angry with what they had done and said, 'Here they are, one people with a single language, and now they have started to do this; now nothing they have a mind to do will be beyond their reach.' So God scattered them from that place and made a confusion of their speech, so that they could not

understand what they said to each other. That place became known as Babel, because God made a babble of the languages of the world. Now God wants you and me and the whole of the Church to work on healing those divisions.

## Hymns and songs

*Come and Praise*
He's got the whole world in his hand (19)
I belong to a fam'ly, the biggest on earth (69)
Make us worthy, Lord (94)

*Hymns Ancient and Modern New Standard*
Christ for the world we sing (344)
Hills of the North, rejoice (470)
Thy kingdom come, O God (177)

*Hymns Old and New: New Anglican Edition*
For the healing of the nations (139)
Inspired by love and anger (252)
Thou, whose almighty word (514)

*Complete Anglican Hymns Old and New*
And ev'ryone beneath the vine and fig tree (774)
Give me peace, O Lord, I pray (802)
The voice from the bush said (896)

*Hymns and Songs for Assembly*
O Lord, all the world belongs to you (83)
O what a wonderful world! (88)
When God made the garden of creation (126)

## Bible readings
*Old Testament – Genesis 11:1-9
New Testament – Acts 2:5-11
Gospel – Mark 16:14-15

## Prayer
Almighty God,
you created the world
and intended all people to live in unity.
Where there is war, bring peace;
where there is hatred, bring love;
where there is anger, bring forgiveness;
for the sake of Jesus Christ,
your Son, our Lord.

## CHILDREN'S WORKSHOP

### Ice-breaker
Bring in a current newspaper or a tape-recording or video of news highlights. Ask the children to note the different places in the world which are mentioned. Look at a globe to find the places. Talk about the things

in the news which should be offered to God in prayers of thanksgiving and intercession.

### Activities
- Make a collage of international news items from various newspapers and add the caption, 'We pray for the world.'
- Invite some people who have lived and worked in other countries to talk about their experience; or those who have taken holidays in other countries to show their photographs. Use an atlas or a globe to find these places and also to locate other places the children know.
- Collect pictures of different places in the world and of different people. These can be stuck to large wall maps of the world. Travel brochures are a good source of such pictures.

### Projects
- Make a display of stamps or flags from around the world, or dolls in traditional dress.
- Make a circle of people of different nationalities holding hands around a picture of the world. Cut out a large circle to represent the world. Colour in land and sea. Cut out figures of people and dress them to represent people from different parts of the world. Arrange the figures around the world.
- Draw up a list of the foods eaten in different parts of the world. Cook and eat some of these foods, or make painted clay models of them. Help the children to realise that not everyone in the world has enough to eat. Make available material from Christian Aid or Oxfam so that children can make realistic comparisons about the amount of food available in different countries.

### Discussion starters
- Look at a globe or world map
- The climate in different countries
- The food grown and eaten in different countries
- The ways of dress in different countries
- the flags of different countries
- ways of praying for the world

### Dance/drama
Use the flags of different nations to devise a dance which begins by emphasising disunity and differences and concludes by emphasising unity and friendship. One way to do this is by beginning with people spaced randomly around the room waving flags in different ways, at different heights, and interfering with each other. By the end of the dance the participants could all be standing in a circle, waving their flags together in such a way that all can be seen equally.

# CELEBRATING TOGETHER

## All-age involvement

Ask members of the congregation to bring along travel brochures, maps and photographs of other countries. Display these, keeping items about each country together, along with a blank sheet of paper for each country. Invite members of the congregation to write on these sheets any items of concern for which you could pray. Use these items in your prayer.

## The service

After the invitation to prayer, ask the congregation to think especially about their responsibility to pray for the world, for the leaders of their own country and for all in positions of authority throughout the world. Draw attention to the activity work and to the topics of intercession and thanksgiving which emerged from the news broadcast and newspapers. It may be appropriate to play back an edited version of the current radio or television news. While the prayer for the world is being offered, the children can hold up their collage of international news items. The children's dance on international diversity and co-operation could be offered before the congregation share in the concluding response to this section of the prayer of the people.

## Display

When we pray for the world, we think of all that God created and everyone for whom Christ died. We need to share in God's care and love for the peoples of the world.

# 14

# Meet the neighbours

## KEY AIMS

- To help children and adults pray for their neighbourhood
- To help the children know their neighbourhood better
- To help the children respect the people who live and work in their neighbourhood
- To help the children be alert to God's care and concern for their neighbourhood

## WORSHIP RESOURCES

### Reference to communion service

*Prayer for our neighbourhood*

When we pray for our neighbourhood, we think of our family, our friends, the individuals within the local community whom we know, those who need our prayers, the many people we don't know and those who have no one to pray for them. We pray for causes of local concern.

### Picture

The picture shows children on their way to school. The crossing patrol woman is there to keep a watchful eye over them. This reminds us of all the people who make a neighbourhood a better place in which to live.

### Bible story

*The Good Samaritan* (Luke 10:29-37)

A teacher of the law asked Jesus the question, 'Who is my neighbour?' Jesus told this story in reply. A man was travelling along the road from Jerusalem to Jericho. Robbers attacked him, stripped him, beat him and went off leaving him half dead. A priest on his way to the temple in Jerusalem came along. He saw the man and went by on the other side. So did a Levite who was also on his way to the temple. Then a foreigner came along, a Samaritan. He saw the man and went across to him. He bandaged his wounds, and carried him on his donkey to an inn where he paid for him to be looked after. 'Now,' said Jesus, 'who do you think was neighbour to the man who fell into the hands of robbers?' Yes, the Samaritan. Now Jesus wants you and me to be like that Samaritan.

## Hymns and songs

*Come and Praise*
In the bustle of the city, there is life (101)
When I needed a neighbour were you there? (65)
Would you walk by on the other side? (70)

*Hymns Ancient and Modern New Standard*
Help us to help each other, Lord (374)
O God in heaven, whose loving plan (407)
Son of God, eternal saviour (132)

*Hymns Old and New: New Anglican Edition*
Brother, sister, let me serve you (73)
Hark, my soul, it is the Lord (197)
Jesus Christ is waiting (268)

*Complete Anglican Hymns Old and New*
Do what you know is right (791)
We turn to you, O God of ev'ry nation (725)
When God made the garden of creation (910)

*Hymns and Songs for Assembly*
Make me a channel of your peace (78)
The world is full of smelly feet (113)
Would you walk by on the other side? (133)

## Bible readings

Old Testament – Leviticus 19:15-18
New Testament – Romans 1:8-10
*Gospel – Luke 10:29-37

## Prayer

Loving God,
you teach us to love all people as our neighbours
and to love our neighbours as ourselves.
Make us alert to the needs of those around us
and help us to be of service to them;
through Jesus Christ our Lord.

## CHILDREN'S WORKSHOP

### Ice-breaker

Prepare a pencil and paper quiz to discover how well the children know their local area. Include street names, names of shops, churches, schools, factories, offices, pubs, the times of buses, the opening hours of libraries, banks and so on. Then encourage the children to talk about all the people who live and work in their neighbourhood. Make a list of the people they mention.

### Activities

- Invite some people who work in the local community to talk about what they do – for example, district nurse, fireman, police officer, postal worker, shopkeeper, etc.
- Take a walk around the local neighbourhood and note all the things of interest. Give special attention to the shops, the places of work and the people.
- Make cut-out pictures of some of the buildings and features of interest in the local community. Assemble them on a coloured background.

### Projects

- Make a map of the local area, showing places of interest.
- Make a collage of those employed in the local community in one way or another – for example, baker, butcher, chemist, crossing patrol person, dentist, district nurse, doctor, dustman, fireman, grocer, hairdresser, milkman, paperboy, policeman, postman, road sweeper, school caretaker, shop assistant, teacher, vicar, etc. Also include those who do voluntary work in the community – for example, the brownie/cub leaders, meals on wheels, Oxfam shop, school governors, etc.
- Produce a guidebook to the local community, giving information for newcomers about churches, schools, shops, doctors, buses, places of interest, etc.

### Discussion starters

- The people and places we pass on the way to school/church
- Local places of work
- Local shops

### Dance/drama

Dress up to represent the many different people in the local community and produce a pageant on the neighbourhood.

# CELEBRATING TOGETHER

### All-age involvement

Invite all members of the congregation to bring something about the local community – for example, the local newspaper, bus timetable, school brochure, shoppers' guide, development plan, photographs of today and of earlier times, etc. Display these objects around the church in thematic groups. Invite some people who work in the local community to talk about what they do – for example, district nurse, fireman, policeman, postman, shopkeeper.

### The service

After the invitation to prayer, invite the congregation to think especially about their responsibility to pray for their neighbourhood, beginning with their own family and friends and embracing all who live and work there. Draw attention to the activity work on local people and places. The children's pageant on the local community could be offered before the congregation share in the concluding response to this section of the prayer of the people.

### Display

When we pray for our neighbourhood, we think of our family, our friends, and all the people who live and work in this area.

# 15

# Sick call

## KEY AIMS

- To help children and adults pray for the sick and suffering
- To help the children feel empathy for those who suffer
- To help the children know about the caring agencies in their area
- To help the children do something practical for their local caring organisations

## WORSHIP RESOURCES

### Reference to communion service

*Prayer for the suffering*

When we pray for the suffering, we think of all those whose grasp on life is threatened in one way or another, by disease, sickness, unhappiness, poverty, mental illness, etc. At the same time we pray for those who are involved with the healing and helping professions.

### Picture

The picture shows people outside the accident and emergency unit of a hospital. A patient is being wheeled in on a bed, while a child is being taken away in a wheelchair. This reminds us of those who suffer and those who care for them.

### Bible story

*Jesus heals a paralysed man* (Mark 2:1-12)

When Jesus came back to Capernaum, news quickly got around about where he was staying. Such a crowd gathered that the door to the house was blocked. Then four men came carrying their paralysed friend on a stretcher in the hope that Jesus would cure him. When they saw that they could not get in through the door, they went up to the flat roof of the house. They broke through the roof covering and lowered their friend down on the stretcher. Jesus saw their faith and said to the paralysed man, 'My son, your sins are forgiven. Stand up, take your bed, and go home.' The man got up, took his stretcher and went out in full view of everyone there. They were amazed and said, 'Never before have we seen anything like this.' Jesus continues to care for the sick and wants us to bring them to him in our prayers, just as those four men brought their friend on the stretcher.

## Hymns and songs

*Come and Praise*
Go, tell it on the mountain (24)
Make me a channel of your peace (147)
O Lord, all the world belongs to you (39)

*Hymns Ancient and Modern New Standard*
Lord Christ, who on thy heart didst bear (388)
O God, by whose almighty plan (406)
Thine arm, O Lord, in days of old (285)

*Hymns Old and New: New Anglican Edition*
At even, ere the sun was set (43)
Go, tell it on the mountain (165)
Lord, we come to ask your healing (319)

*Complete Anglican Hymns Old and New*
A brighter dawn is breaking (3)
All of the people on the mountain (772)
Christ is our king (784)

*Hymns and Songs for Assembly*
Give us hope, Lord, for each day (32)
Jesus' hands were kind hands (64)
Make me a channel of your peace (78)

## Bible readings

Old Testament – Ecclesiasticus 38:1-8
New Testament – James 5:13-16
*Gospel – Mark 2:1-12

## Prayer

Almighty God,
your Son Jesus Christ healed the sick
and brought them to wholeness of life.
Where there is pain, bring healing;
where there is sickness, bring health;
where there is unhappiness, bring hope;
that all may share Christ's risen life,
who reigns with you and the Holy Spirit,
now and for ever.

## CHILDREN'S WORKSHOP

### Ice-breaker

Invite a nurse or doctor from the congregation to come to talk with the children about their work. Ask them to show the children some of the tools of their trade, such as a thermometer, stethoscope, and doctor's bag. Encourage the children to talk about the various caring professions and groups which serve the local community and make a list of them: doctors, dentists, opticians, nurses, ambulance drivers, school nurse, Red Cross, St John Ambulance, etc.

## Activities

- Make get-well greetings cards to send to any members of the local church who are ill.
- Collect advertisements for plasters and medicines and make a display of them.
- Write a diary entry for the paralysed man healed by Jesus in Mark 2:1-12.

## Projects

- Arrange a visit to a local hospital, dentist or doctor's surgery. Perhaps members of the congregation who work in these places can arrange this and talk to the children beforehand.
- Make a collection of toys to take to the children's ward of the local hospital or a large mural to display in the hospital. Check first that the hospital would welcome such initiatives. Discover if the hospital is doing anything special to raise funds, like running a fête or a car boot sale. Plan how you can become involved. Alternatively, plan a visit to a local retirement home to put on a concert.
- Make a poster showing all the people involved in the local hospital. The central illustration is a patient in bed. Around this patient are the surgeon, radiographer, staff nurse, sister, doctor, porter, anaesthetist, cleaner, cook, ward clerk, student nurse, physiotherapist, maintenance staff, ambulance driver, GP, hospital administrator, pharmacist, etc. Decide how to make all these people distinctive.

## Discussion starters

- Feeling ill
- Going to the doctor, hospital, dentist
- Visiting people who are sick
- What it feels like to be housebound and frail

## Dance/drama

Sharpen the children's awareness of specific disabilities by role play. Ask them to imagine that they are blind, deaf, lame, etc., and to act out the consequences of that disability and the way in which they can strive to overcome it.

# CELEBRATING TOGETHER

## All-age involvement

Around the walls place sheets of paper, each headed with a medical worker in your local community – for example, GP, physiotherapist, osteopath. (Include a few blank sheets in case you have forgotten some groups.) Place underneath each a sheet of adhesive coloured dots. Invite members of the congregation to walk around the building, placing a dot on the page of each profession that has helped them in the past two years. Think about what these dots show of the need in our lives of medical help and support. Pray, naming all these groups.

## The service

After the invitation to prayer, invite the congregation to think especially about their responsibility to pray for those who are sick or who are suffering in body, mind or spirit, and for those involved in the caring and helping professions. Draw attention to the activity work and describe any contact that they have had with the local hospital, etc. Invite the congregation to pray for individual people by name and remind them of the intercession board.

## Display

When we pray for the suffering, we think of all who are sick in body, mind or spirit. We also pray for those concerned with the healing and helping professions.

# 16
# Light and life

## KEY AIMS

- To help children and adults appreciate the fellowship of the saints in their prayers
- To help the children explore the image of light
- To help the children experience their continuity with their own church in earlier ages
- To help the children know something about the saints

## WORSHIP RESOURCES

### Reference to communion service

*Prayer for the departed*

The final section of the prayer of the people suggests three ideas: commemoration of the departed, bringing the departed to mind before God, which may include specific people mentioned by name; thanksgiving for the lives and witness of the saints, which may include mention of specific saints; and commendation of the worshippers and all Christian people to God. The saints have been lights to the Church in their different generations.

### Picture

The picture shows a host of burning candles, with all their flames flickering in the same direction. This picture speaks to us of the saints who have been lights to the Church in their different generations.

### Bible story

*Called to be saints* (Matthew 5:1-12)

The word *saint* means *holy*. The saints of God are holy people. They are not people who lived a long time ago and in far-off places. They are not people who wear haloes on their heads and smile out from stained glass windows. They are people who have responded to God's call to live holy lives in God's service. In Matthew's Gospel, Jesus paints a picture of those who are called to be saints. He says:

Happy are those who know their need of God.
Happy are those who are sorrowful for their sins.
Happy are those who live gentle lives.

Happy are those who hunger and thirst to see right done.
Happy are those who show mercy to others.
Happy are those who have pure hearts.
Happy are those who make peace.
Happy are those who suffer persecution because they stand for what is right.

Jesus speaks these words to you and me as much as to the saints of old. We are called to be saints.

## Hymns and songs

*Come and Praise*
Colours of day dawn into the mind (55)
From the darkness came light (29)
The bell of creation is swinging for ever (86)

*Hymns Ancient and Modern New Standard*
For all the saints who from their labours rest (305)
Glory to thee, O God (363)
Lord God, we give you thanks for all your saints (488)

*Hymns Old and New: New Anglican Edition*
Come, let us join our cheerful songs (94)
Hark! the sound of holy voices (200)
In our day of thanksgiving (247)

*Complete Anglican Hymns Old and New*
Jesus bids us shine (845)
O when the saints go marching in (876)
Ye watchers and ye holy ones (758)

*Hymns and Songs for Assembly*
A new commandment (7)
Lord, the light of your love is shining (75)
This little light of mine (118)

## Bible readings

Old Testament – 2 Esdras 2:42-48
New Testament – Hebrews 11:13-16 and 12:1-2
*Gospel – Matthew 5:1-12

## Prayer

Almighty God,
you have called people to your service in every age.
Help us to follow in the footsteps of your saints,
that we may share with them Christ's risen life,
who reigns with you and the Holy Spirit,
now and for ever.

# CHILDREN'S WORKSHOP

## Ice-breaker

Assemble pictures, photographs or postcards of a number of local churches dedicated to different saints. See how many of the churches the children recognise and how many of the names they know. Talk about why churches are dedicated to saints and draw out the children's idea of who the saints are. Look at stained glass windows and pictures of the saints. Especially draw attention to some of the apostles. Develop the idea that the saints were real men and women and not simply pictures in stained glass. They were and continue to be 'lights' to the Church.

## Activities

- Write a poem on the beatitudes from Matthew 5:1-12.
- Make decorative candles, using cardboard tubes or paper cylinders and tissue paper for the flame. You may like to write a name on each candle, the name of someone you consider to be a 'light' to the Church.
- Produce large posters about the four Gospel writers: Matthew is represented by a man; Mark is represented by a winged lion; Luke is represented by a winged ox; John is represented by a rising eagle.

## Projects

- Make real candles. Your local library or bookshop should have books giving detailed instructions, including safety procedures when dealing with hot wax.
- Write and draw about some of the people who have been associated with your church in the past, using information such as the memorial tablets in the church, the list of past churchwardens and vicars, the church guidebook, etc.
- Make stained glass windows of saints from cellophane or tissue paper. Use thin black paper strips to make a frame and the outline of your picture. Then glue pieces of coloured cellophane or tissue paper to the back of the black paper. (Rest the work on plastic supermarket bags. When the glue dries, the bag can be peeled away.) When completed, display on a clear window for the sun to shine through.

## Discussion starters

- Look at a lighted candle and talk about it
- How are candles used in churches and why?
- The people associated with your church in the past
- The churchyard and the people buried there
- The saints in history and legend

## Dance/drama

Develop a mime about being in darkness and the gradual lighting of more and more candles. Let the children use the candles they have made.

# CELEBRATING TOGETHER

## All-age involvement

Invite members of the congregation to bring candles. Place extra candles around the church near any memorial plaques or stained glass windows picturing the saints. Reflect on the way our faith has been passed on to us. Light a taper from the altar candle and use this to light the candles around the church. Invite people to light their own candles from those around the church or from others in the congregation.

## The service

After the invitation to prayer, invite the congregation to think especially about the final section of the prayer of the people. Remind them how around the eucharist they are one with the whole Church of Christ, living and departed. Draw their attention to the activity work on light and on the saints. While this section of the prayer is being offered, the children can hold up their banners. If the children have developed a mime on light, using the candles they have made, this can be presented immediately before the congregation share in the concluding response of the prayer of the people.

## Display

In the eucharist the whole Church of Christ, living and departed, is united. We share our celebration with all the saints.

# 17
# Say it with hands

## KEY AIMS

- To help children and adults understand the significance of the Peace
- To help the children explore ways in which hands are creative
- To help the children explore ways in which hands express feelings and communicate them to others
- To help the children want to be peacemakers

## WORSHIP RESOURCES

### Reference to communion service

*Peace*

The Peace brings to a climax the Ministry of the Word and initiates the Ministry of the Sacrament. The Peace proclaims restored relationships between the fellow members of the congregation and symbolically includes the idea of our intended reconciliation with all people. The placing of the Peace immediately before the offertory is influenced by Matthew 5:23-24. In many churches the words of the Peace are accompanied by a hand clasp as we stretch out our hands to receive another person into the community of peace.

### Picture

The two pictures illustrate the power of hands to bind people together and to proclaim peace. In one picture the hands bind together the adults, the child, and the baby. In the other picture two hands (of different colours) stretch out to welcome and to receive each other.

### Bible story

*Jesus tells us to make peace* (Matthew 5:9, 23-24)

St Matthew tells us how Jesus taught his disciples and the crowds in his famous Sermon on the Mount. One of the things Jesus said was this: 'How happy are the people who make peace. God shall call them his sons and daughters.' Then Jesus went on to explain how much God values people who make peace. He said, 'If you are bringing your gift to God's altar and suddenly remember that you are angry with someone, leave your gift where it is. First go and make peace with that person and then come back and offer your gift.' That is why we share the peace in church before offering our gifts to God on the altar.

## Hymns and songs

*Come and Praise*
I belong to a fam'ly (69)
Shalom, shalom, may peace be with you (141)
We are climbing Jesus' ladder (49)

*Hymns Ancient and Modern New Standard*
Hands that have been handling (278)
In Christ there is no east or west (376)
Lord of all hopefulness, Lord of all joy (394)

*Hymns Old and New: New Anglican Edition*
Peace is flowing like a river (412)
Peace, perfect peace in this dark world (413)
Peace, perfect peace is the gift (414)

*Complete Anglican Hymns Old and New*
Peace, perfect peace in this dark world (554)
Peace to you (556)
Take my hands, Lord (624)

*Hymns and Songs for Assembly*
Jesus' hands were kind hands (64)
Peace, perfect peace (91)
Shalom, my friends (101)

## Bible readings

Old Testament – Isaiah 9:6-7
New Testament – 1 Thessalonians 5:23-28
*Gospel – Matthew 5:23-24

## Prayer

Almighty God,
your Son proclaimed peace to his followers.
Give us your peace in our lives
that we may learn
to forgive with hope,
share with joy
and serve with love.
We make our prayer
in the name of the Prince of Peace.

## CHILDREN'S WORKSHOP

### Ice-breaker

Spread out some wrapped sweets on a table, so that there are more sweets than children. Then ask the children to put their hands on their heads and to help themselves to one sweet. Discuss the difficulty they experience when they are not allowed to use their hands. Then draw out from them all the other ways in which hands are essential or useful. Include a discussion on how hands are used to greet people and to make friends.

### Activities

- Make a chain of hands to stretch right round the inside of the church. Make handprints by covering hands in paint and pressing on paper.
- Set up a bright light and explore the use of hands to make shadow puppets.
- Produce pictures showing how hands can communicate feelings and intentions: a clenched fist indicates anger; a wave indicates greeting or farewell; a handclasp indicates pleasure or victory; holding hands indicates friendship.

### Projects

- Produce a poster showing the children and the whole congregation exchanging the sign of peace in the communion service. It may be easiest to plan your poster together, and then to assign each pair of children two figures. The figures can be drawn on separate pieces of paper then cut out and assembled. If you want a poster which will show up clearly you may want to make figures one-quarter life-size. You could use fabric for clothes and wool for hair.
- Look at the episodes in the Gospels which mention Jesus' hands. Explore how Jesus used his hands to express God's goodwill towards people. Draw pictures of some of these episodes and make them into a book. You may like to draw each picture inside a hand shape. Some episodes are:
  – Jesus beckons Simon and Andrew to follow him (Mark 1:16-18)
  – Jesus takes Simon's mother-in-law by the hand and heals her (Mark 1:29-31)
  – Jesus lays his hands on the children (Matthew 19:13-15)
  – Jesus feeds the crowd (Mark 6:41-44)
  – Jesus heals the blind man (Mark 8:22-26)
  – Jesus washes the disciples' feet (John 13:5-9)
  – Jesus breaks bread (Mark 14:22-23)
  – Jesus blesses the disciples (Luke 24:50-51)
- Watch people who are skilled with their hands – for example, a furniture restorer, a potter, someone embroidering or making corn dollies or origami. Learn some simple techniques and let the children experiment and be creative.

### Discussion starters

- The things we make with our hands
- The people who use their hands to help us
- The way we greet people and say goodbye with our hands
- The sign language used by the deaf
- Hand puppets

### Dance/drama

Develop a series of short mimes on the theme of 'What's my line?' when the children are allowed to communicate only through gestures with their hands.

# CELEBRATING TOGETHER

## All-age involvement

Invite members of the congregation to bring along pictures or objects that symbolise peace in some way. Display these. Ask people to individually shape their hands into a sign of peace, and then ask them to work with those around them to shape a group of hands into a symbol of peace.

## The service

Before the Peace draw the congregation's attention to the activity work on hands. If the children have prepared mime on the theme of 'What's my line?', invite the congregation to try to guess the themes being mimed. Then have space for an extended peace with the congregation moving around to greet as many people as possible with a hand clasp.

## Display

At the Peace we show our intention to accept and welcome each other as followers of Christ. The outward sign of our intention is the hand clasp.

# 18

# Shopping spree

## KEY AIMS

- To help children and adults understand the significance of the offertory
- To help the children see in the bread and wine symbols for all God's gifts and human work
- To help the children be aware of their dependence on God as the origin of everything
- To give the children the opportunity of expressing gratitude to God for all God's gifts

## WORSHIP RESOURCES

### Reference to communion service

*Preparation of the gifts*

The gifts of the people are brought to the altar before the Eucharistic Prayer. Two kinds of gifts are involved, different in their meaning and significance. First, the people present the bread and wine of the eucharist, symbols of the fruit of the earth and the work of human hands. Second, the people give money, a symbol of their commitment to the needs of the Church and of the world.

### Picture

The picture shows a shopping trolley full of different foods. This reminds us that the bread and the wine brought to the altar in the eucharist symbolise so much more, in terms of the fruit of the earth and the work of human hands.

### Bible story

*King David praises God* (1 Chronicles 29:10-13)

King David decided to build a grand temple for God in the city of Jerusalem. He gave a lot of his own wealth towards the temple and invited other people to do the same. Many people gave very generously. When King David dedicated all their gifts to God he composed this great hymn of praise:

Blessed are you, Lord God of Israel.
Yours, Lord, is the greatness,
the power, the glory, the splendour, and the majesty;
for everything in heaven and on earth is yours.

We remember King David's words when we bring our gifts of bread and wine to the altar.

## Hymns and songs
*Come and Praise*
I will bring to you the best gift I can offer (59)
Lord of the harvest (133)
Thank you, Lord, for this new day (32)

*Hymns Ancient and Modern New Standard*
Almighty Father, Lord most high (267)
Praise and thanksgiving (415)
Reap me the earth as a harvest to God (507)

*Hymns Old and New: New Anglican Edition*
God, whose farm is all creation (179)
Praise, O praise our God and King (423)
We plough the fields and scatter (534)

*Complete Anglican Hymns Old and New*
Now join we, to praise the creator (471)
Praise God for the harvest of orchard and field (559)
We eat the plants that grow from the seed (904)

*Hymns and Songs for Assembly*
Give thanks for the sun, the wind and the rain (74)
Pears and apples, wheat and grapes (92)
We can plough and dig the land (122)

## Bible readings
*Old Testament – 1 Chronicles 29:10-13
New Testament – 1 Corinthians 16:1-3
Gospel – Luke 12:32-34

## Prayer
Almighty God,
all things come from you.
We praise you for your goodness.
Help us to use your gifts properly,
for our own well-being,
for the help of those in need
and for your glory;
through Jesus Christ our Lord.

## CHILDREN'S WORKSHOP

### Ice-breaker
Borrow a shopping trolley from a local store and ask the children to bring empty packets, jars and bottles to fill the trolley. Ask the children to write a shopping list and then to compare notes. Talk about all the different things in the trolley and on the shopping list: where they have

come from, how they are made, where they are grown. See how the 'fruit of the earth' and the 'work of human hands' are represented in so many different things and in so many different ways.

### Activities

- Involve the children in making some foods, which they usually see only in their processed and packaged state, from the raw materials. For example, make some homemade sweets, or make butter out of cream. If you have enough time you could bake bread or biscuits.

- Make a collection of pictures of food being grown in different areas or countries.

- Bring in the communion chalice (cup) and paten (plate) for the children to examine. Let them sketch these, paying attention to all the details. If you have church catalogues, look at other designs available. Remember that the bread and wine are symbols of God's gifts and of human work.

### Projects

- Arrange a visit to a local shopping centre and invite the manager from a local store to show the children around and to talk about his or her work. Prepare a map of the local shopping area, making a list of what is available from each shop. Draw pictures of some of the local shops.

- Create a 'supermarket' in part of the church. Paint posters and advertisements for the supermarket. Make a checkout point.

- Trace the processes involved in manufacturing some foods. Try to acquire information from the manufacturers and create project books or wall charts on a few items.

### Discussion starters

- Local shops which sell food, and other things
- Food grown in local gardens, allotments, fields
- Food processed in local factories
- The work involved in producing some everyday foods and drinks – for example, crisps and coffee

### Dance/drama

Write hymns of praise to God, like King David's great hymn. Help the children to interpret these through choral speech and mime.

# CELEBRATING TOGETHER

## All-age involvement

Invite all members of the congregation to bring 'some shopping' to the church with them, preferably non-perishable goods. Either display these goods at the front of the church, or collect them in supermarket trolleys to be pushed up the aisle during the offertory procession. Arrange beforehand whether these items are to be donated to a local charity, auctioned at the end of the service, or sold from a market stall in the town during the coming week.

## The service

Before the preparation of the gifts, invite the congregation to see their gifts of bread and wine as symbols for all the fruit of the earth and the work of human hands. Draw attention to the activity work and to the shopping brought to church by the congregation. If these gifts have been placed in supermarket trolleys, incorporate these trolleys in the offertory procession. If the children have prepared choral speech and mime this can be presented at the climax of the preparation of the gifts.

## Display

At the preparation of the gifts we bring bread and wine to the altar as symbols of all the fruit of the earth and of all the work of human hands.

# 19
# Bird watching

### KEY AIMS

- To help children and adults explore the preface to the Eucharistic Prayer
- To help the children enjoy studying birds
- To help the children see the bird as a symbol for the Holy Spirit
- To help the children appreciate the presence of the Holy Spirit in the eucharist

### WORSHIP RESOURCES

#### Reference to communion service

*Preface to the Eucharistic Prayer*

Literally 'eucharist' means giving thanks. Here in the opening dialogue the president invites the people to 'give thanks to the Lord our God'. By their assent the people are associated with this thanksgiving from the very beginning. In the Eucharistic Prayer the people of God affirm that 'The Lord is here' and 'His Spirit is with us'.

#### Picture

The picture shows a large friendly bird hovering over the world, over the land, and over the sea. This reminds us how Scripture often visualises the Holy Spirit as a bird, as is the case, for example, in the baptism of Jesus in Matthew 3.

#### Bible story

*The Holy Spirit at Jesus' baptism* (Matthew 3:13-17)

Before he began his work of teaching and healing, Jesus was baptised by John the Baptist. Jesus came to the River Jordan, where John was teaching, and he saw John baptise a number of people. John was dressed in a rough coat of camel's hair and wore a leather belt around his waist. Jesus asked John to baptise him. John led Jesus into the river so that the water completely covered him. When Jesus came up out of the water, the Holy Spirit came down like a dove and rested on him. A voice from heaven said, 'This is my Son.'

## Hymns and songs

*Come and Praise*
Morning has broken (1)
Spirit of peace, come to our waiting world (85)
There is singing in the desert (26)

*Hymns Ancient and Modern New Standard* E.H.
Alleluia, sing to Jesus! (262)  − 271
Christian people, raise your song (443)
Lord Jesus Christ (391)  297

*Hymns Old and New: New Anglican Edition*
An upper room did our Lord prepare (29)
Jesus is Lord! (270)
Jesus, stand among us (279)

*Complete Anglican Hymns Old and New*
At the Lamb's high feast we sing (53)
Come, risen Lord (126)
Jesus calls us here to meet him (346)

*Hymns and Songs for Assembly*
All over the world (4)
Spirit of God (102)
Spirit of peace, come to our waiting world (103)

## Bible readings
Old Testament – Genesis 1:1-5
New Testament – Acts 2:1-4
*Gospel – Matthew 3:13-17

## Prayer
Almighty God,
your Holy Spirit was active
to create the world,
to baptise your Son
and to empower the disciples.
Strengthen us by your Holy Spirit,
to proclaim your praise
and to live to your glory;
through Jesus Christ our Lord.

## CHILDREN'S WORKSHOP

### Ice-breaker

Take the children outside to observe birds in the local neighbourhood (they need to be very quiet and binoculars might help); or bring a budgerigar in a cage; or find large pictures of birds. Encourage the children to talk about the different kinds of birds found locally, their song, how they fly, where and how they build their nests, how they feed their young, where they go in winter and so on. Some children may have seen birds in an aviary, a zoo or a park.

### Activities

- Produce a bird mobile which can be hung in the church. You could choose to have several birds of the same design, or different designs for each bird. You will need to experiment to find the best position on the bird for tying the string; it needs to be a central position for the bird to hang freely. For a three-dimensional bird, cut out a shape with beak and tail. Make cuts in the tail for a feather effect. Make a vertical cut in the body and press through paper that has been folded like a fan. Open out the folded paper to make wings either side of the body.

- Listen to bird song and try to imitate it. Some music and songs imitate birds, like the hymn 'From out of the wood did the cuckoo fly.'

- Explore the local church to see if the symbol of the bird appears there. See especially the font cover, stained glass, lectern, etc.

### Projects

- Produce a book about birds in the local community. You will need to spend time birdwatching. Include the location where you found the birds, their habits, their sounds, the time of day you are most likely to find them, etc. You could go to a local park and quietly observe birds, counting how many you see of each variety.

- Produce a set of banners showing the Holy Spirit active throughout history – for example:
  - *Creation*: Show how the world looked before civilisation, including the dove and the text 'The Holy Spirit was at work in creation.'
  - *Jesus*: Portray the baptism of Jesus, including the dove and the text 'The Holy Spirit was at work in Jesus.'
  - *Early Church*: Portray the day of Pentecost, including the dove and the text 'The Holy Spirit was at work in the early Church.'
  - *Eucharist*: Portray the altar, including the dove and the text 'The Holy Spirit is at work in the communion.'

- Visit a local art gallery to find the symbol of the bird in Christian art. Paint pictures of Bible scenes, showing the presence of the Holy Spirit through the symbol of a bird.

### Discussion starters

- Birds in the local neighbourhood, pigeons around the church
- Birds at the seaside, seagulls
- Birds kept as pets, budgerigars and parrots
- Birds seen at the zoo
- Patterns of bird migration
- Pictures of birds in Christian art

### Dance/drama

Develop a dance about bird flight to appropriate music.

# CELEBRATING TOGETHER

## All-age involvement

Invite members of the congregation to join you in a tour of your building, both inside and outside, looking for signs and inscriptions that remind you of the presence of the Holy Spirit. At each one you could stop and say, 'The Lord is here: His Spirit is with us.' If your congregation is very large, you may prefer to do this in smaller groups so that people do not feel left out.

## The service

Before the Eucharistic Prayer, invite the congregation to think about the importance of the bird as a symbol for God the Holy Spirit. Draw their attention to the activity work about birds. If the children have prepared dance about bird flight, this can be shared. If they have made banners, these can be held up throughout the Eucharistic Prayer.

## Display

The beginning of the Eucharistic Prayer reminds us that the Holy Spirit is present in the eucharist. The same Holy Spirit is at work in creation, in Jesus and in his followers. In Christian art the Holy Spirit is often represented by the bird.

# 20

# Journey into space

### KEY AIMS

- To help children and adults respond to the majesty of God in the 'Holy, holy, holy Lord'
- To help the children explore the greatness and wonders of the planets and space
- To help the children appreciate the greater wonder of God as creator of the planets and space
- To help the children discover that space travel does not conflict with the Christian's faith, but makes us more aware of God's greatness

### WORSHIP RESOURCES

#### Reference to communion service

*Holy, holy, holy Lord*

In the Eucharistic Prayer we join with angels and archangels in a great shout of praise. This shout uses two ancient hymns. The first – 'Holy, holy, holy Lord' – echoes passages of Scripture like Revelation 4:8 and Isaiah 6:3. The second – 'Blessed is he who comes' – echoes passages like Psalm 118:26 and Mark 11:9-10. Both hymns emphasise the majesty and otherness of God.

#### Picture

The picture shows a vast night sky stretching over the expanse of earth and sea. This reminds us of the magnitude and sheer wonder of the world that we inhabit. The ancient song, 'Holy, holy, holy Lord', is the appropriate human response to such transcendence.

#### Bible story

*The mighty sun* (Psalm 19:1-6)

When the writer of the psalms looked up into the sky, he saw the sun, moon, stars and planets. It seemed that all these great lights in the sky were singing and shouting God's praises. So he wrote this great hymn of praise to God who made them all:

The heavens above shout God's praises:
the great lights tell out what he has made.
The sun wakes up in the morning
like a strong man ready to run his race.
He rises at one end of the heavens,
travels right across the sky
and sets in the farthest west.
Nothing is hidden from his light.
The heavens above shout God's praises:
the great lights tell out what he has made.

(From the *Good News Bible*)

## Hymns and songs
*Come and Praise*
All creatures of our God and King (7)
By brother sun who brings the day (78)
He's got the whole world in his hand (19)

*Hymns Ancient and Modern New Standard*
Eternal ruler of the ceaseless round (353)
Every star shall sing a carol (354)
Let all mortal flesh keep silence (256)

*Hymns Old and New: New Anglican Edition*
All heav'n declares (14)
Holy, holy, holy (212)
Hosanna, hosanna (215)

*Complete Anglican Hymns Old and New*
Have we made our God too small (815)
Holy, holy, holy is the Lord (285)
Think big: an elephant (899)

*Hymns and Songs for Assembly*
O Lord, my God, when I, in awesome wonder (84)
Praise him on the trumpet (93)
Wide, wide as the ocean (132)

## Bible readings
*Old Testament – Psalm 19:1-6
New Testament – Revelation 4:6-11
Gospel – John 1:1-5

## Prayer
Holy, holy, holy Lord,
you are Lord of earth and sea,
you are God of sun and moon.
Holy, holy, holy Lord,
you are Lord of stars and planets,
you are God of all there is.
Holy, holy, holy Lord.

# CHILDREN'S WORKSHOP

## Ice-breaker

Watch a short extract from a science fiction video about space travel. Select an episode which emphasises the mystery and wonder of the spaceship and the vastness of space rather than the drama of war and conflict! Ask the children to discuss their ideas about space and space travel.

## Activities

- Compose hymns of praise to God. Use imagery from Psalm 19, the sun and space travel.
- Make a huge sun to hang in the church. Cover it with gold paper and sprinkle it with glitter. You might like to write inside it 'Holy is the Lord'.
- Make space helmets for the children to wear.

## Projects

- Make a spaceship control station.
- Make suns on poles for the children to hold up and process. You could let each child make a sun or they could work in pairs. Use cardboard shapes covered with shiny paper and glitter. Attach the poles firmly so the suns do not slip during the procession.
- Make sundials and at regular intervals ask the children to note the place of the shadow so you can mark it. Alternatively, make a large shadow clock in a field or playground and mark the shadow with string and pegs (field) or chalk (playground). You will find information about sundials in your local library or bookshop.

## Discussion starters

- Recent films, videos or television programmes about science fiction journeys into space
- The sky at night
- The sun and a list of its influences – for example, light, heat, suntan, growth, shadows, etc.
- Space rockets

## Dance/drama

The theme of space travel produces many ideas for drama and dance – for example, life at the rocket launching station, launching the rocket, life in the space capsule, landing on the moon, the eerie exploration of an unknown planet.

# CELEBRATING TOGETHER

## All-age involvement

Invite all members of the congregation to assemble material which speaks to them of the wonder of space and the majesty of God. This may include music, pictures, poetry and prose. Give opportunity for small groups to discuss what each person has brought. Display the pictures, read two or three of the poems and listen to an example of music. Then allow these to be reflected on in silence.

## The service

Before the Eucharistic Prayer, invite the congregation to think about the great feelings of mystery, awe and praise evoked by the 'Holy, holy, holy Lord'. Draw their attention to the activity work on the sun and on the journey into space. If the children have made suns on poles these can be processed while the congregation is singing or saying the 'Holy, holy, holy Lord'. If they have written hymns on the sun or prepared suitable dance, these can be shared immediately after the 'Holy, holy, holy Lord'.

## Display

The great shout 'Holy, holy, holy Lord' reminds us of the greatness and majesty of God. If we are overwhelmed by the vastness of outer space and by the greatness of the sun, how much more are we overwhelmed by the God who made the whole universe.

# 21

# Wedding reception

## KEY AIMS

- To help children and adults recognise the Last Supper in the eucharist
- To help the children explore the celebration of a wedding reception
- To help the children see the significance of sharing a wedding cake
- To help the children discover the events of the Last Supper

## WORSHIP RESOURCES

### Reference to communion service

*Institution Narrative*

The Institution Narrative relates the account of the origin of the Eucharist during Jesus' Last Supper with his twelve disciples. Jesus instructed his followers to 'do this in remembrance of me'. This account is at the centre of the Eucharistic Prayer. Some of Jesus' parables help us to see the eucharist as a great wedding banquet.

### Picture

The picture shows the priest presiding at the altar on which the girl is placing bread and the boy is pouring wine. The picture speaks to us of the great wedding banquet over which Christ presides in the kingdom of God, and we are invited to share in that banquet.

### Bible story

*The Last Supper* (Mark 14:12-16, 22-25)

The Passover is a great festival for the Jewish people. They meet together for a meal in the evening and as they eat the special food they tell the great tale of how God rescued them from being slaves in Egypt. Jesus arranged to celebrate the Passover meal with his 12 disciples in a large upstairs room. During the supper, Jesus took bread, he said the blessing, broke the bread and he shared it with the disciples. He said, 'Take this; this is my body.' Then he took a cup, said the blessing and shared it with them. He said, 'Drink this; this is my blood.' We repeat Jesus' actions and words at the Passover meal every time we celebrate communion.

## Hymns and songs

*Come and Praise*
Now the harvest is all gathered (139)
Said Judas to Mary (28)
There's a child in the streets (27)

*Hymns Ancient and Modern New Standard*
Dear Lord, to you again our gifts we bring (352)
O holy Father, God most dear (410)
O thou who at thy Eucharist didst pray (265)

*Hymns Old and New: New Anglican Edition*
At the Lamb's high feast we sing (45)
Jesus took a piece of bread (281)
Love is his word, love is his way (332)

*Complete Anglican Hymns Old and New*
As we break the bread (48)
Gifts of bread and wine, gifts we've offered (200)
God of the Passover (228)

*Hymns and Songs for Assembly*
Lord Jesus Christ, you have come to us (72)
Said Judas to Mary (98)
We have a King who rides a donkey (123)

## Bible readings

Old Testament – Exodus 12:14-17
New Testament – 1 Corinthians 11:23-26
*Gospel – Mark 14:12-16, 22-25

## Prayer

Lord Jesus Christ,
at the Last Supper
you took bread and blessed it,
you broke bread and shared it.
As we do this in remembrance of you,
may we know your risen power in our lives
and share in your eternal kingdom,
where you live and reign
now and for ever.

## CHILDREN'S WORKSHOP

### Ice-breaker

Make a small wedding cake, sponge rather than fruit, appropriately
decorated. Welcome the children to a wedding reception. Encourage
them to talk about their experience of weddings and wedding receptions.
Provide a veil for a bride and a hat for a groom and invite the children to
take it in turns to preside at cutting the cake. Share the cake.

## Activities

- Decorate a wedding cake to eat yourselves or to share with the congregation. The cake will need to be cooked in advance. You may choose to make individual small cakes instead of one large cake, so that each child has a cake to decorate.
- Arrange to hold an agape with the children and with their families, when an evening meal is shared and the eucharist is celebrated as part of the meal. Discuss arrangements for it and make invitations.
- Write a letter from one of Jesus' disciples to a friend, describing the events of the Last Supper.

## Projects

- Discuss who was present at the Last Supper and produce a mural showing the table, the food and the disciples. Each child could draw one or two figures.
- Plan a wedding reception, prepare the food and invite the congregation to share in it during or after the Sunday service. Make wedding cards and appropriate decorations for the wedding reception. Include horse-shoes, bells, paper flowers, etc.
- Learn about the ways that people from different denominations celebrate the eucharist or communion. Look for the parts in every service that are based on the Last Supper. Prepare descriptions or service sheets for each one, highlighting the similarities.

## Discussion starters

- Weddings attended by the children, seen in the local church, seen on television
- Pictures of the Last Supper
- Wedding cakes and decorations
- Sending pieces of cake to those who cannot attend the wedding so they can share in the celebration
- Looking at a family wedding photograph album

## Dance/drama

Develop a short play or dance about a wedding service and the reception.

# CELEBRATING TOGETHER

## All-age involvement

Invite members of the congregation to bring along photographs of weddings at which they have been guests. In buzz groups they can show these photographs to each other, tell one special feeling related to the wedding, and then tell a special feeling related to attendance at the eucharist.

## The service

After the 'Holy, holy, holy Lord' invite the congregation to think about the importance of the Passover meal in shaping the Eucharistic Prayer. Invite them also to contemplate the eucharistic imagery of the wedding banquet. If the children have made a poster about the Last Supper, this can be displayed while the Institution Narrative is recited. If the children have prepared a wedding reception, the congregation can be invited to share in this after the service.

## Display

While celebrating the Passover meal with his disciples, Jesus gave a new significance to the bread and to the wine. Every time the eucharist is celebrated we share with Jesus in that great meal.

# 22

# Bread and wine

## KEY AIMS

- To help children and adults perceive how bread and wine speak to the Christian community about the presence of Christ
- To help the children study the history of a loaf of bread
- To help the children study the history of a bottle of wine
- To help the children perceive how bread and wine speak about the people and processes involved in their production

## WORSHIP RESOURCES

### Reference to communion service

*Acclamation*

The Acclamation, like the 'Holy, holy, holy Lord' earlier, is an ancient Christian hymn. Its place in the Eucharistic Prayer provides an opportunity for the people to offer their assent to what has gone before. In some liturgies the people are specifically invited to join in the Acclamation through an invitation to 'proclaim the mystery of faith'. Now the bread and the wine speak to the worshipping community of the body and blood of Christ.

### Picture

The picture now focuses our attention on the key outward signs of the Sacrament of Holy Communion, on the bread and on the wine. The special significance of these everyday essentials of food and drink is emphasised by the brilliant shafts of light.

### Bible story

*Jesus shares bread with his friends* (Luke 24:28-32)

After Jesus rose from the dead on Easter Sunday, he met two of his disciples as they were walking along the road away from Jerusalem to Emmaus. They did not know Jesus had risen from the dead. They were sad and did not even recognise him. But because it was growing late, they invited this stranger to stay with them. When Jesus sat down with them for a meal, he took the loaf of bread. He said the blessing. He broke the bread and he shared it with them. In the sharing of the bread they recognised Jesus was with them. In the eucharist we, too, do those four things: we take the bread; we say the blessing; we break the bread; we share the bread. In the sharing of the bread we know that Christ has died, Christ is risen and Christ will come again.

## Hymns and songs

*Come and Praise*
Thank you, Lord, for food to eat (32)
The earth is yours, O God (6)
When from the sky in the splendour of summer (132)

*Hymns Ancient and Modern New Standard*
Come, risen Lord, and deign to be our guest (349)
My God, and is thy table spread (259)
Praise and thanksgiving (415)

*Hymns Old and New: New Anglican Edition*
Alleluia, sing to Jesus (26)
I am the bread of life (222)
Let us talents and tongues employ (301)

*Complete Anglican Hymns Old and New*
Christ is alive! Let Christians sing (96)
Farmer, farmer, why do you plough (796)
Lord of the future, Lord of the past (862)

*Hymns and Songs for Assembly*
Lord Jesus Christ (72)
Lord, the light of your love is shining (75)
There is singing in the desert (111)

## Bible readings
Old Testament – Psalm 104:13-15
New Testament – Acts 2:42-47
*Gospel – Luke 24:28-32

## Prayer
Lord Jesus Christ,
we praise you for your gift of bread:
for seed time and harvest,
for sun and rain,
for miller and baker.
Lord Jesus Christ,
we praise you for the gift of yourself:
made known to us
in the breaking of bread.

## CHILDREN'S WORKSHOP

### Ice-breaker
Bring a fresh and attractive looking loaf of bread. Break it and share it with the children. Invite them to describe what it tastes like and to talk about all the people and processes involved in its manufacture, and

draw up a list. Bring some red grape juice and pour it into an attractive beaker. Share it with the children. Invite them to describe what it tastes like and to talk about all the people and processes involved in its manufacture, and draw up a second list.

### Activities

- Invite someone who is good at making bread to talk about the process and to bring along ingredients plus prepared bread dough to show. Together mix some bread dough, then leave it aside to rise. Take the already prepared and risen dough and shape it into rolls or a loaf. Perhaps this could be taken home and cooked, then frozen and brought back the following week to use in the eucharist and for sharing after the eucharist.

- Invite someone who is keen on wine making to talk about his or her hobby, bringing in ingredients plus wine at various stages to show. Together take part in some of the processes, either making wine from real fruit and flowers (blackberries, apples, dandelions or elderflowers) or from a tinned concentrate prepared for wine making.

- Visit a flour mill, a baker or a farm which grows wheat.

### Projects

- Produce a book telling the history of a loaf of bread. Different children can contribute different sections – for example, grain is delivered to the farm, fields are ploughed, seeds are sown, crops are sprayed, rain falls and sun shines, the corn is harvested and threshed and dried, grain is transported to the mill, grain is ground into flour, flour is transported to the baker, dough is prepared, loaves are baked, bread is bought in the shops, bread is eaten in many different forms, bread is taken in the eucharist.

- Produce a book telling the story of a bottle of wine. Different children can contribute different sections – for example, vines are planted, vines are tended, rain falls and sun shines, grapes are picked, juice is extracted, the fermentation process begins, the wine matures, the wine is bottled, the bottles are displayed in the shops, wine is consumed, wine is taken in the eucharist.

- Make salt dough models of the bread and wine used in the eucharist. (Make salt dough by mixing together 1 cup salt, 1 cup water, 3 cups flour and a dribble of cooking oil. Knead the dough for two minutes then leave it for 30 minutes before shaping. Bake small models for one hour at gas mark 2, 150°C or 300°F, and large models for three hours at gas mark 1, 135°C or 275°F. Paint the cooked models and varnish them with PVA glue.)

### Discussion starters

- The different types of bread in local shops, supermarkets and bakers
- The many different forms in which we eat bread
- The local wine shops and the different types of bottles
- The occasions when people drink wine
- The kind of bread and wine used in the eucharist
- The children's experience of baking bread or making wine at home

### Dance/drama

Develop a dance to tell the life story of a loaf of bread. Include sowing the seed, the grain growing, cutting the corn, grinding the flour, kneading the dough. Bring the dance to a climax with the bread being used in a feast and in the eucharist.

## CELEBRATING TOGETHER

### All-age involvement

Display bread in a variety of forms – for example, rolls, sandwich loaves, round loaves, fruit loaves, continental loaves, pitta bread. Invite members of the congregation to discuss which form of bread they use most often, and when they use the less common forms. Then hold up the communion bread and remind the congregation of this special form of bread, and the special occasion on which it is used.

### The service

Before the offertory, draw the congregation's attention to the activity work on bread and wine. If the children have made bread and wine, incorporate this in the offertory procession. Use some of their bread for the eucharist and invite the congregation to stay afterwards to share the loaves. If the children have prepared dance, this can be celebrated at the point of the Acclamation.

### Display

In the Acclamation 'Christ has died, Christ is risen, Christ will come again' we proclaim our faith that Christ is present with us through the bread and wine of the eucharist.

# 23

# Carnival time

## KEY AIMS

- To help children and adults experience the Eucharistic Prayer as a time of celebration
- To help the children explore the idea of carnival time
- To help the children enter into the joy of carnival time
- To help the children be alert to the joy of the Eucharistic Prayer

## WORSHIP RESOURCES

### Reference to communion service

*Thanksgiving and Doxology*

The Eucharistic Prayer concludes with a great shout of praise. Eucharist itself means thanksgiving, so it is most appropriate that the Eucharistic Prayer should end on a high note. The mood is one of joy and of carnival, of thanksgiving in the presence of the risen Christ. Remembrance of Christ's saving actions in the past culminates in the joyful celebration of his saving presence. Solemnity and celebration merge.

### Picture

The picture shows children waving colourful banners as the great Eucharistic Prayer of thanksgiving reaches its climax. The banners carry many of the traditional symbols of the Christian Church, including the cross, the dove, the fish, the boat, the lamb, and the chi-rho. This reminds us that the eucharist is a real celebration of joy.

### Bible story

*The crowds welcome Jesus with palm branches* (Matthew 21:6-11)

On Palm Sunday Jesus rode into Jerusalem on a donkey to show the people that he was a gentle leader, not a war-like warrior. The crowds gathered around him and went wild with excitement. Some people took off their cloaks to make a royal carpet for him to ride on. Others cut branches from the trees to spread in his path. They all raised the shout, 'Blessings on him who comes in the name of the Lord.' We, too, can raise that shout of praise and wave our arms and banners when we meet with Christ in the eucharist.

## Hymns and songs

*Come and Praise*
All creatures of our God and King (7)
O Praise him! (13)
Rejoice in the Lord always (95)

*Hymns Ancient and Modern New Standard*
Hills of the north, rejoice (470)
Lord enthroned in heavenly splendour (263)
Thine be the glory, risen, conquering Son (428)

*Hymns Old and New: New Anglican Edition*
Fill thou my life, O Lord my God (129)
Give thanks with a grateful heart (154)
God is our strength from days of old (171)

*Complete Anglican Hymns Old and New*
All of my heart, all of my soul (770)
All the nations of the earth (773)
Clap your hands, all you people (785)

*Hymns and Songs for Assembly*
Come on and celebrate! (20)
O what a wonderful world! (88)
Praise him on the trumpet (93)

## Bible readings

Old Testament – Psalm 148:1, 7-14
New Testament – Revelation 5:11-14
*Gospel – Matthew 21:6-11

## Prayer

Lord Jesus Christ,
you came into Jerusalem
riding on a donkey.
The crowds praised your holy name
and waved branches in the air.
Lord Jesus Christ,
you come among your people
in the bread and in the wine.
We glorify your holy name
and sing your praises for ever.

## CHILDREN'S WORKSHOP

### Ice-breaker

Choose a well-known local carnival or fair and try to find photographs of it, perhaps from local newspapers. Encourage the children to talk about their experiences of this carnival or fair. Build a picture of the various things that take place and the aspects which most appeal to individual children. Explore the reasons why people like carnivals and fairs.

## Activities

- Make a range of paper or cardboard banners to process and hold during the Thanksgiving and Doxology. Prepare the banner shapes in advance so that you have time to decorate them together. Begin by asking the children what they think ought to be on the banners and flags they bring to the eucharist. Ideas might include:
  - texts – for example, Alleluia, Jesus is Lord, Praise him
  - pictures – for example, Easter Tomb, Jesus talking to the crowds, bread and wine
  - Christian symbols – for example, cross, fish, dove, chalice, ship, lamb, chi-rho
- Make palm branches to wave in celebration or to decorate your walls.
- Choose appropriate percussion instruments (or make your own) and plan when they can be used in this part of the Eucharistic Prayer to show celebration.

## Projects

- Produce a large mural of a carnival, asking each child to make something for it. The mural might include a band, drum majorettes, people in fancy dress, clowns, decorated floats, a procession of vintage cars, etc. The procession might be moving towards a fairground, including stalls, side shows, and amusements like dodgems and the big wheel.
- Make a model of a fairground, the type associated with a carnival.
- Arrange for the children actually to take part in a local carnival, perhaps involving a decorated float or fancy dress. Bring their preparation to the eucharist.

## Discussion starters

- Local fairs and carnivals
- Banners and the signs carried in processions
- Carnivals in other parts of the world
- Medieval fairs

## Dance/drama

Develop a short play or dance based on the story of Jesus entering into Jerusalem on the donkey.

# CELEBRATING TOGETHER

## All-age involvement

Invite all members of the congregation to think about a carnival or similar occasion which they have experienced and enjoyed, perhaps in their childhood, perhaps on a visit overseas, or perhaps a recent local event. Some may be able to bring photographs of these occasions. Make an opportunity to share these memories and to display the pictures.

## The service

Before the Eucharistic Prayer, invite the congregation to think about the Thanksgiving and Doxology as a great shout of praise. Draw attention to the activity work on carnival time. Use the story of Palm Sunday to help link the ideas of praise and carnival. If the children have made banners these can be processed or held high during the Thanksgiving and Doxology.

## Display

The Eucharistic Prayer concludes with a great shout of praise. Our celebration can be expressed as a carnival held in honour of the presence of the risen Christ.

# 24

# Picnic time

### KEY AIMS

- To help children and adults use the Lord's Prayer as part of their own prayer life
- To help the children enjoy picnics
- To help children understand communion as a special meal for the family of God
- To help the children enrich their understanding of the family prayer

### WORSHIP RESOURCES

#### Reference to communion service

*Lord's Prayer*

The Lord's Prayer is placed after the Eucharistic Prayer and before the distribution of communion. A number of early Church fathers saw this as an appropriate place for the Lord's Prayer because of the petition 'Give us this day our daily bread' which some of them interpreted as meaning the bread of the eucharist. It is also natural for the people of God to share in their family prayer before coming to the family table.

#### Picture

The picture shows children enjoying a picnic as they take part in an extended family meal. This is a highly appropriate context in which to share the family prayer of the Church. The picture also gives special point to the words, 'Give us today our daily bread.'

#### Bible story

*Jesus teaches his disciples to pray* (Luke 11:1-4)

St Luke tells us that Jesus often spent time alone in prayer. His followers saw this and asked Jesus to teach them how to pray. They said, 'John the Baptist taught his followers to pray. Teach us how to do so as well.' Jesus answered like this. 'When you pray say:

Our Father in heaven,
hallowed be your name,
your kingdom come,
your will be done,
on earth as in heaven.

Give us today our daily bread.
Forgive us our sins
as we forgive those who sin against us.
Lead us not into temptation
but deliver us from evil.'

Because Jesus taught this special prayer to his followers we know it as the 'Lord's Prayer' and as the family prayer of the Church. Today we share this family prayer with Christians throughout the world.

## Hymns and songs

*Come and Praise*
Come, my brothers, praise the Lord (20)
Our Father, who art in heaven (51)
The Lord, the Lord, the Lord is my shepherd (108)

*Hymns Ancient and Modern New Standard*
Bread of heaven, on thee we feed (271)
Let us talents and tongues employ (481)
Who are we who stand and sing? (529)

*Hymns Old and New: New Anglican Edition*
O thou, who at thy Eucharist didst pray (391)
Our Father, who art in heaven (411)
Praise to the Lord (427)

*Complete Anglican Hymns Old and New*
Come, O Lord, inspire us (124)
Forgive our sins as we forgive (180)
Thy kingdom come, O God (691)

*Hymns and Songs for Assembly*
Abba, Father, let me be (1)
Father, I place into your hands (23)
Father, we love you (26)

## Bible readings

Old Testament – Exodus 16:14-18
New Testament – Romans 8:14-16
*Gospel – Luke 11:1-4

## Prayer

Lord God,
your Son Jesus Christ
showed us we belong to your family
and taught us to call you Father.
Help us to know your presence
as we share your family meal
of bread and wine;
through Jesus Christ our Lord.

# CHILDREN'S WORKSHOP

## Ice-breaker

Arrange a simple picnic and find somewhere enjoyable to share it with the children. Or bring a picnic hamper and unpack it with the children, encouraging them to talk about what is in it. Draw out from the children their own experiences of picnics. Give attention to the food, the family atmosphere and the fun of the picnic.

## Activities

- Produce a list of all that is required for a picnic: the different foods, the drinks, the cups and plates. Models can be made of all these things from plasticine, clay, or cardboard.

- Make a poster of special meals – for example, birthday food, family celebrations, communion, school end-of-year parties. Remind the children that communion is a special meal for the family of God.

- Look at the different versions of the Lord's Prayer in Matthew 6:9-13 and Luke 11:1-4. Copy out these different versions and also copy out the different versions of the Lord's Prayer used in church services.

## Projects

- Some children may like to produce a richly illuminated text of the Lord's Prayer to display in the church.

- Produce a sequence of murals telling the story of a teddy bears' picnic, from the time the teddy bears get up in the morning to the time they return home. Include any special songs or poems the teddy bears might use.

- Prepare a teddy bears' picnic which the group can share with younger children in church. Make a large backcloth, showing trees, grass, flowers, toadstools, perhaps a castle or a house. A foreground also needs to be made, perhaps using imitation grass. Trees, flowers, benches and fallen logs can also be part of the foreground. A large and welcoming sun can be fixed in the sky. Signs can be arranged around the building pointing to 'Teddy Bears' Picnic Area'. Prepare food for the teddy bears' picnic, including biscuits baked to look like teddy bears. Bring or make teddy bears.

## Discussion starters

- Places the children have been for picnics
- Food they have enjoyed eating on picnics
- Special things they do at picnics, such as family songs or poems
- A teddy bears' picnic
- Talk about the different ideas in the Lord's Prayer:
  - God cares (our Father)
  - God reigns (your kingdom come)
  - God provides (give us today)
  - God forgives (forgive us)
  - God protects (lead us not)
  - God is praised (for the kingdom)

### Dance/drama
Make teddy bear masks or costumes and devise a dance to the children's song 'The Teddy Bears' Picnic'.

## CELEBRATING TOGETHER

### All-age involvement
Invite members of the congregation to think about special family sayings or songs they use. These could be written out in advance and displayed. Give each family a sheet of stickers and ask them to put one sticker next to each saying they use, to see how many are general sayings and how many are unique. Hold up a copy of the Lord's Prayer and introduce it as a special prayer for the family of God.

### The service
Before the Lord's Prayer encourage the congregation to think about the relationship between the family prayer and the family meal. Introduce them to the activity work on the picnic and draw out the parallels between picnic time and eucharist. If the children have prepared a teddy bears' picnic, the setting can be arranged early during the Ministry of the Word and the teddy bears can be brought to share their picnic immediately before the Lord's Prayer.

### Display
The Lord's Prayer is the family prayer of the Church. We pray this prayer together as a family just before we share in the family meal of the eucharist.

# 25

# Fair shares

## KEY AIMS

- To help children and adults understand 'breaking the bread' as a symbol of Christian sharing
- To help the children explore ways of sharing
- To help the children become more aware of the diversity of needs around them
- To help the children become aware of some Third World needs

## WORSHIP RESOURCES

### Reference to communion service

*Breaking the bread*

When a real loaf of bread is used for the eucharist, this liturgical act of breaking the bread serves the practical function of dividing the loaf into suitable size pieces for distribution. It also has the important symbolic function of demonstrating the unity of the people of God who share in the one loaf. In early Christian thought the same Greek word, *koinonia*, was used to convey the three ideas of sharing, fellowship and communion. All these ideas are summed up in breaking the bread.

### Picture

The picture shows the priest breaking the communion bread so that everyone present can share it. This speaks to us of the command to share our resources in the kingdom of God.

### Bible story

*Food is shared among 5000 people* (Mark 6:35-44)

Sometimes great crowds of people followed Jesus out of the towns and villages to hear him teach. One day the crowd had grown to about 5000. Towards the evening the disciples interrupted Jesus and said, 'It is getting late and these people are a long way from home. Send them off to get something to eat.' Jesus, however, told the disciples to see how much food they had to hand. They produced five loaves of bread and two small fishes. Jesus ordered the people to sit down on the green grass in groups of about 100. Then Jesus took the loaves; he said the blessing; he broke the loaves; he shared the loaves among the disciples; and he told the disciples to distribute the pieces to the crowd. Everybody ate to their heart's content and there was still some left over. In the eucharist we, too, share loaves of bread with Jesus and with all his disciples throughout the ages.

## Hymns and songs

*Come and Praise*
O Lord, all the world belongs to you (39)
Sad, puzzled eyes of small hungry children (74)
When God made the garden of creation (16)

*Hymns Ancient and Modern New Standard*
Bread of the world in mercy broken (270)
Come, risen Lord, and deign to be our guest (349)
Let us break bread together on our knees (480)

*Hymns Old and New: New Anglican Edition*
Bread is blessed and broken (66)
Broken for me (72)
This is my body, broken for you (506)

*Complete Anglican Hymns Old and New*
Bread of the world in mercy broken (83)
Break the bread and pour the wine (780)
From many grains, once scattered far and wide (196)

*Hymns and Songs for Assembly*
I give my hands (48)
I'm going to paint a perfect picture (55)
Pears and apples, wheat and grapes (92)

## Bible readings
Old Testament – Isaiah 58:6-7
New Testament – 1 Corinthians 10:16-17
*Gospel – Mark 6:35-44

## Prayer
Eternal God,
your Son Jesus Christ broke bread
to feed a hungry people
and to bring new life
to a broken world.
When we break bread in his name,
fill us with his life
and send us out
to share his love with others.

## CHILDREN'S WORKSHOP

### Ice-breaker
For a group of 12 children, before the class begins take a relatively simple jigsaw puzzle and divide the pieces into four bags. Divide the class into groups of three and give a bag of pieces to each group. Invite all the

groups to try to make a picture out of their pieces. Gradually bring the groups together to discover how they need each other's pieces to construct the picture. As you work discuss the importance of sharing and co-operation. Draw out ideas of frustration and incompleteness without co-operation and sharing.

### Activities

- Make a list of all the different people who have recently contributed to the lives of class members, from the obvious ones like the school teacher, to the less obvious like the people who cut down the tree to make the paper they are writing on.

- Explore some of the needs of the Third World. Make use of recent materials produced by missionary societies or world development organisations, or invite someone who has worked in the Third World to talk about their work and to show pictures, films, artefacts, etc.

- Write or draw about Jesus feeding the 5000 people. You could write a diary entry or a letter from one of the people, talking about hunger followed by the relief of food when Jesus shared out the bread and fish.

### Projects

- Develop a wall chart or project book on the theme 'We share in each other's work'. Include, for example, public services (water, electricity, gas, sewage, refuse collection), communications (post, telephone, buses, trains), health service (doctors, dentists, nurses), social services (home helps, job centres, meals on wheels), distribution services (lorry drivers, shopkeepers, milk delivery), food production (farmers, bakers, packaging and processing plants), consumer production (toy makers, car manufacturers, furniture makers).

- Arrange a fundraising event so that the children can contribute directly to a missionary society or world development organisation.

- Produce a book called 'Sharing the world's resources'. Glue into this labels of foods, clothes, etc., showing their origin in other parts of the world.

### Discussion starters

- The children's own experiences of sharing
- How we benefit from the work of others
- How we benefit from food produced in other parts of the world
- How we can share our resources with others

### Dance/drama

Develop a short play about the feeding of the 5000.

# CELEBRATING TOGETHER

## All-age involvement

Before the service display information about different needs in our country and around the world, and information about what the church is doing to help. Separate into small groups, each to investigate one of these needs and responses. A representative from each group reports back a two-sentence summary of this information to the congregation, finishing with the words 'We are the body of Christ.' The congregation responds 'Though we are many, we are one body.'

## The service

Before 'breaking the bread' draw the congregation's attention to the activity work on sharing. Invite the children to talk about their experience of sharing the pieces of the jigsaw puzzle. If the children have prepared drama on the feeding of the 5000, this can be shared at this stage of the service. On this occasion it might also be helpful to defer the Peace until this stage of the service (where it is placed in the Roman Catholic rite) to symbolically involve the whole congregation in the drama of feeding the 5000.

## Display

Breaking the bread reminds us how Jesus shared food with the 5000 people. We, too, need to share our resources with God's people throughout God's world.

# 26
# Pilgrim way

### KEY AIMS

- To help children and adults explore the Invitation to Communion
- To help the children think about journeys
- To help the children explore the part played by journeys and pilgrimages in the Christian tradition
- To help the children appreciate the Invitation to Communion as a pilgrimage for the people of God

### WORSHIP RESOURCES

#### Reference to communion service

*Invitation and administration*

The words of Invitation are addressed to the whole people at once. The response of the people is to make pilgrimage to the point where communion is distributed. It is customary in many churches for those who are not yet admitted to receive communion to make pilgrimage to the point of distribution to receive a blessing.

#### Picture

The picture shows the child being invited to draw near in faith to share in the sacrament of bread and wine. The invitation calls out a response as the child leaves her seat and begins the pilgrimage to the altar rail.

#### Bible story

*Moses meets with God* (Exodus 3:1-6)

When Moses was a young man he worked for his father-in-law Jethro as a shepherd. One day he was out with the sheep near Mount Horeb, which is known as 'the mountain of God'. Suddenly Moses noticed a bush which was on fire but which was not being burnt up. Looking at the bush Moses became aware that God was there with him and talking to him. He took off his shoes as a sign of reverence and covered his face because he was afraid to gaze on God. When we come to the eucharist, we know that God is with us in the bread and in the wine, just as Moses knew he was there in the burning bush. Like Moses, we want to draw near to God with reverence.

He who valiant be## Hymns and songs

*Come and Praise*
He who would valiant be (44)
There is singing in the desert (26)
Time is a thing (104)

*Hymns Ancient and Modern New Standard*
And now, O Father, mindful of the love (260)
Dear Lord, to you again our gifts we bring (352)
Lord Jesus Christ (391)

*Hymns Old and New: New Anglican Edition*
Gather around, for the table is spread (152)
Jesus took a piece of bread (281)
Lift high the cross (303)

*Complete Anglican Hymns Old and New*
Forward in faith, forward in Christ (800)
Step by step, on and on (885)
We pray thee, heav'nly Father (720)

*Hymns and Songs for Assembly*
Riding out across the desert (96)
Travel on, travel on, there's a river that is flowing (119)
We are marching in the light of God (4)

## Bible readings
*Old Testament – Exodus 3:1-6
New Testament – 1 Corinthians 11:18-21
Gospel – Matthew 8:5-8

## Prayer
Come, Lord Jesus,
stand among us in the bread and wine.
Come, Lord Jesus,
draw us near to your table.
Come, Lord Jesus,
live in us and stay with us.
Come, Lord Jesus, come.

## CHILDREN'S WORKSHOP

### Ice-breaker
Encourage the children to talk about journeys they have undertaken and enjoyed. Draw out the places to which they have made journeys and their reasons for doing so – for example, to see Granny, to go to a certain shop, to spend time at the seaside. Then show them pictures of events and places to which Christians make journeys or pilgrimages – for example, the local cathedral and the events which happen there, local diocesan days arranged for children and families, a shrine like Walsingham and the Spring Bank Holiday national pilgrimage. Discuss why Christians make journeys to these places.

## Activities

- Make a display about pilgrimages to the Holy Land. Collect appropriate material from church newspapers and church travel agencies and organisations. Invite someone who has made a pilgrimage to the Holy Land to bring pictures. Alternatively make a display about a contemporary place of pilgrimage, like Canterbury Cathedral or the shrine of Our Lady of Walsingham.

- Write a series of 'Prayers for the Pilgrims at Communion'. Prayer 1 could be for people sitting or kneeling at their seats before coming to the altar. Prayer 2 could be for people walking from their seats on the pilgrimage to communion. Prayer 3 could be for people receiving communion or being blessed at the altar.

- Produce costumes or head-dresses for the children to dress as 'pilgrims throughout the ages', including figures like Abraham, the medieval pilgrims to Canterbury, the Pilgrim Fathers and contemporary pilgrims. You could use material, paper and cardboard.

## Projects

- Discuss Abraham, who responded to God's call, set out from his home and risked the unknown to seek a new place in which to serve God. Produce a large collage of Abraham, his family and servants, his tents and his flocks of sheep.

- Discuss the Pilgrim Fathers, who risked their lives sailing to a strange land in order to find a new home where they could serve God as they thought right. Produce a mural of their ship and figures of the Pilgrim Fathers in their characteristic dress.

- Arrange for the children to participate in a pilgrimage to a place like Walsingham or to visit a medieval place of pilgrimage like Canterbury. Before the pilgrimage you will need to explain to the children what they will see. Afterwards, plan a display of photographs, leaflets, drawings, models, etc.

## Discussion starters

- Journeys the children have experienced
- Pilgrimages
- The children's experience of the distribution of communion in their own church and in other churches
- Ways of showing reverence to the presence of Christ in the eucharist
- Signs of reverence before the sacrament, like genuflection
- How people use the time of the administration in personal devotion

## Dance/drama

Develop a short play about people preparing to go on a pilgrimage, perhaps discussing where they will go, what they will do, and what they need to take.

## CELEBRATING TOGETHER

### All-age involvement

If any members of the congregation have been on a pilgrimage, invite them to speak for a maximum of two minutes on a topic such as preparing for the pilgrimage, stages on the way, changes in attitude as they journeyed, etc. Together take a mini pilgrimage around the church grounds as a preparation for communion.

### The service

After the 'breaking the bread' invite the congregation to think of their journey to the altar rail as a kind of pilgrimage. Draw attention to the activity work on the pilgrim way. If the children have prepared costumes or head-dresses characterising pilgrims throughout the ages, these can be worn by the children (and by adults) as they make their own pilgrimage to the altar rail.

### Display

We are invited to draw near with faith and to receive the sacrament. We respond by making a pilgrimage to the altar. There we meet with Christ in a special way.

# 27

# Birthday invitation

## KEY AIMS

- To help children and adults explore the 'Prayer of Humble Access'
- To help the children understand the significance of being invited to a birthday party
- To help the children 'feel at home' at a birthday party as a consequence of being invited
- To help the children feel at home around God's table because they know that God himself has invited them

## WORSHIP RESOURCES

### Reference to communion service

*Prayer of Humble Access*

This prayer is based on the Prayer of Humble Access composed by Thomas Cranmer for the 1548 *Order of Communion*. It was designed to help the congregation to share in, and prepare themselves for, further participation in the eucharist. As we look forward to receiving the sacrament we remind ourselves that we come to God's table not because we are worthy to do so but because God himself is kind enough to invite us.

### Picture

The picture shows the family seated round the table at meal time. The family dog is there with them waiting for crumbs from the table. This reminds us that we are all called and welcome to share at God's table.

### Bible story

*Jesus eats with Zacchaeus* (Luke 19:1-10)

Zacchaeus lived in Jericho. He was a Jew but had turned traitor by working for the Roman authorities. He collected taxes from the Jews to help pay for the Roman army. His fellow countrymen hated him. When Jesus came to Jericho, Zacchaeus, who was very short, climbed into a tree to see him. Jesus spoke kindly to Zacchaeus and invited Zacchaeus to eat with him. The crowds were shocked that Jesus shared a table with a man like Zacchaeus. We, too, are not worthy of Jesus' company, but Jesus specifically invites us to share his table.

## Hymns and songs
*Come and Praise*
God is love; his the care (36)
Join with us to sing God's praises (30)
You shall go out with joy (98)

*Hymns Ancient and Modern New Standard*
Christians, lift your hearts and voices (447)
Come let us join our cheerful songs (144)
Come, risen Lord, and deign to be our guest (349)

*Hymns Old and New: New Anglican Edition*
Among us and before us (28)
Author of life divine (48)
Dearest Jesus, we are here (107)

*Complete Anglican Hymns Old and New*
Lord, we come to ask your healing (422)
Our God loves us (548)
The table's set, Lord, your people gathered (668)

*Hymns and Songs for Assembly*
Father welcomes all his children (25)
I'm accepted, I'm forgiven (52)
Little children, come to me (25)

## Bible readings
Old Testament – Proverbs 9:1-6
New Testament – Hebrews 10:19-23
*Gospel – Luke 19:1-10

## Prayer
Lord Jesus Christ,
you invite us to your table.
We are not fit even to eat the crumbs,
but your love welcomes us and draws us in.
Give us grace to accept your invitation
and to eat and drink with you,
in your eternal kingdom.

## CHILDREN'S WORKSHOP

### Ice-breaker
Prepare individual invitations addressed personally to each of the children inviting them to a special celebration, perhaps a party for the Sunday school or a short gathering after church. If possible, post these during the preceding week. Encourage the children to talk about their feelings

on receiving the invitation: excitement, anticipation and the feeling of being personally invited by name. You only go to a party when you have been invited. Encourage them to talk about their experiences of birthday parties, etc.

### Activities
- Write invitations to members of the congregation, inviting them to share a small celebration with the children after the service. Prepare party food to share with the congregation at the celebration. Make party hats to help people 'feel at home' at the celebration.
- Design invitations to members of the congregation to meet together around God's table in communion.
- Work out actions to accompany the Prayer of Humble Access. Thinking about actions will enable the children to understand the prayer.

### Projects
- Make a large mural showing the setting for a children's party. Begin with a large table and invite each child to contribute a picture of party food to glue on to the table. Then let the children draw pictures of themselves and add these pictures to the mural. Each child's portrait can be named, perhaps by adding party hats bearing their names. In order to make the party more of a 'family affair', ask the children if they would wish to invite adults and pets as well. Add to the mural pictures of parents, grandparents, godparents, Sunday school teachers and pets (all suitably labelled). The mural can have the heading 'We have all been invited to the party'.
- If you have access to a digital camera and a computer, prepare a PowerPoint presentation about responding to God's invitation to communion. Photographs could include the invitation from the altar, the children (and any available adults) responding individually, the group together at the altar rails. Each photograph will need a simple phrase or sentence to accompany it.
- Interview Zacchaeus and the people in the crowd about their reaction to Jesus' invitation. The interview could be recorded by video camera or cassette tape.

### Discussion starters

- Planning a party and inviting guests
- Making party food
- Organising party games
- Welcoming party guests
- Writing thank you letters

### Dance/drama

Act out the story of Jesus going to Jericho, seeing Zacchaeus up the tree and eating with Zacchaeus.

# CELEBRATING TOGETHER

## All-age involvement

Invite members of the congregation to bring along an invitation which has been important to them – for example, an invitation to a wedding, a new job, or a committee. Some people may prefer to bring a photograph or other souvenir of the occasion. Display these. Ask a few people to talk about these invitations and their feelings at receiving them. Add to the display an invitation to God's table.

## The service

Before the Prayer of Humble Access, ask the congregation to think about the way in which Jesus invites them to share his table. If the children have been preparing for a celebration immediately after the service, ask them to give an invitation card personally to everyone in church. If the children have prepared drama on the theme of Zacchaeus, this can be presented before the whole congregation joins in the Prayer of Humble Access.

## Display

The Prayer of Humble Access reminds us that we are not worthy to eat the crumbs under Jesus' table. Yet he invites each one of us to eat and drink with him.

# 28

# Known by name

## KEY AIMS

- To help children and adults to explore the words of Administration
- To help children reflect on the significance of their own name
- To help children to know that God calls and invites them by name
- To help children hear their own name when the word 'you' in the Administration is addressed to them individually

## WORSHIP RESOURCES

### Reference to communion service

*The body of Christ keep you in eternal life*

Throughout the communion service, until this point, so much of the emphasis has been on the whole worshipping community, the people of God, acting together. In the confession *we* have confessed *our* sins. In the creed *we* have confessed *our* faith. Now in the Administration each person is addressed individually as the bread is placed in her hands or as the wine passes his lips. The 'you' spoken now is heard afresh as if spoken directly and specially to each individual. Sometimes those authorised to administer the sacrament make this point more explicit by addressing the individual communicants by name. Indeed, some large congregations make this possible by inviting members of their congregation to wear a name badge.

### Picture

The picture shows children and adults kneeling before the altar to receive communion. The space in the picture between the individuals emphasises how each individual is addressed by name and, consequently, invited to make an individual response to God.

### Bible story

*The birth of John the Baptist* (Luke 1:5-25, 57-66)

Names are important to God. Here is a story about how one of God's prophets got his name. Zechariah was a priest who served God in the temple. He and his wife Elizabeth were getting quite old and were sad that they had no children. God chose them to be the parents of John the Baptist who was sent to prepare the way for Jesus. One day when Zechariah was in the temple, the angel Gabriel appeared to him and said, 'Do not be afraid, Zechariah; your prayer has been heard. Your wife Elizabeth will bear you a son, and you are to give him the name John.' When the child was born, everyone wanted to name him after his father and call him Zechariah. But Elizabeth and Zechariah spoke up. 'No,' they said, 'he is to be called John.' And it was so.

## Hymns and songs

*Come and Praise*
God who made the earth (10)
He's got the whole world in his hand (19)
I belong to a fam'ly, the biggest on earth (69)

*Hymns Ancient and Modern New Standard*
Here, O my Lord, I see thee face to face (274)
Let all mortal flesh keep silence (256)
My God, and is thy table spread (259)

*Hymns Old and New: New Anglican Edition*
And now, O Father (32)
Be still, for the presence of the Lord (53)
James and Andrew, Peter and John (257)

*Complete Anglican Hymns Old and New*
Do not be afraid, for I have redeemed you (150)
Gather around, for the table is spread (199)
Sweet sacrament divine (622)

*Hymns and Songs for Assembly*
Be still, for the presence of the Lord (13)
I'm black, I'm white, I'm short, I'm tall (54)
There are hundreds of sparrows (109)

## Bible readings
Old Testament – 1 Samuel 3:1-10
New Testament – Acts 9:10-17
*Gospel – Luke 1:57-66

## Prayer
Lord Jesus Christ,
you call us by name
to become your disciples.
We follow you.
Lord Jesus Christ,
you call us by name
to eat in your kingdom.
We praise you,
now and always.

# CHILDREN'S WORKSHOP

## Ice-breaker

Help each child to make a simple cardboard crown and to write their name in big letters on the crown. Then invite the children to wear their crowns and to take it in turn to say to the whole group, 'My name is N, and I am important to God.'

## Activities

- Organise 26 sheets of paper round the room, one for each letter of the alphabet. Now invite the children to think of as many names as possible to write on each sheet.

- Create a poster of famous people, using pictures from magazines. Provide a caption for each person in the picture, such as 'My name is John.'

- Look through the telephone directory to discover the family names in your area which take up at least two pages. Create a poster with a heading like, 'The most popular names in my area are Evans, Jones, Thomas, and Williams.'

## Projects

- Produce a series of pictures telling the story of the birth of John the Baptist. Show the angel Gabriel appearing to Zechariah. Show Elizabeth nursing the baby boy. Show the crowd pressing for the boy to be called Zechariah after his father. Show Zechariah insisting, 'He is to be called John.' These pictures should be on poster paper, large enough to be displayed around the walls when finished. The children can work in pairs or small groups on each picture. You will need to decide on details such as hair colouring or clothing, so it is similar in all pictures.

- Ask the children to find out about their own name. How did their parents choose their name? See if they can find out what their name means. Do they share their name with famous or important people? Create a class book called 'My name'.

- Create a book for each child in the group. The book could be titled 'A book about Sian', and each page could have a heading such as 'My name is Sian'. Each page could give a different piece of information, like family details, favourite food and drink, appearance, favourite activities, something that is important.

## Discussion starters

- How do you feel when the minister places the bread in your hand and says, 'The body of Christ keep you in eternal life'?
- How do you like your name?
- Who else do you know who is called by your name?

## Dance/drama

Develop a dance sequence to express the experience of Zechariah. After the angel had appeared to him, Zechariah lost his ability to speak until his son was born and he had kept the command to give him the name of John.

## CELEBRATING TOGETHER

### All-age involvement

Invite the members of the congregation to bring a name badge with them. They may decide whether they want to be known as Mrs Smith, Jane Smith, or Jane. Invite some of the adults to come forward and to introduce themselves to the children by name. In buzz groups talk about the importance of knowing that God knows each one of us by name.

### Service

Before the people begin to leave their seats to come up to receive communion, discuss with them the significance of God addressing each one of us by name in the administration of the sacrament. For today's service ask the communicants to say their name to the minister before the bread is placed in their hands. Instruct the minister to use the form of administration, 'Jane, the body of Christ keep you in eternal life.'

### Display

When the bread of communion is placed in our hands, God is addressing us individually. God knows each of us by name.

# 29

# Come dancing

## KEY AIMS

- To help children and adults express gratitude to God for the eucharist
- To help the children explore ideas of dance and movement
- To help the children express thanks to God with their bodies
- To help the children explore reasons for thanking God

## WORSHIP RESOURCES

### Reference to communion service

*After communion*

After communion a short prayer sums up our gratitude to God. We thank God for feeding us in the eucharist, and then ask to be sent out in the power of the Holy Spirit to live and work to God's praise and glory. The depth of thanksgiving can be expressed not only in words, but also in movement and dance.

### Picture

The picture shows children with arms outstretched dancing around the priest. The eucharist is coming to a close and now priest and people are thanking God for feeding them in the sacrament. They are giving thanks both with the words of their mouths and the movements of their bodies.

### Bible story

*The healed man dances God's praise* (Acts 3:1-8)

Every day the crippled man was to be seen lying by the temple gate in Jerusalem, to beg money from those who passed by. He was so crippled his friends had to carry him there each morning. One day he saw the two apostles, Peter and John, and asked them for money. Peter replied, 'I do not have any money. But what I have I will give to you. In the name of Jesus Christ of Nazareth, get up and walk.' With that Peter helped the man to get up and the man found that he could walk. He was so excited he went into the temple with Peter and John, walking, leaping, dancing and praising God. After God's great gift to us in the eucharist, we too should say thank you with our whole being. And sometimes this can mean leaping and dancing as well as singing.

## Hymns and songs

*Come and Praise*
Autumn days when the grass is jewelled (4)
In the bustle of the city (101)
Think of a world without any flowers (17)

*Hymns Ancient and Modern New Standard*
I danced in the morning (375)
Praise the Lord, rise up rejoicing (416)
Stand up, and bless the Lord (201)

*Hymns Old and New: New Anglican Edition*
Dance and sing all the earth (105)
God is good, we sing and shout it (168)
In the Lord I'll be ever thankful (250)

*Complete Anglican Hymns Old and New*
Clap your hands and sing this song (786)
Dance in your Spirit (140)
Oh, I could sing unending songs (823)

*Hymns and Songs for Assembly*
Jesus put this song into our hearts (66)
Praise the Lord in the rhythm of your music (94)
There is singing in the desert (111)

## Bible readings

Old Testament – Psalm 149:1-5
*New Testament – Acts 3:1-8
Gospel – Luke 17:12-18

## Prayer

Lord Jesus Christ,
we shout your praise;
accept our words.
Lord Jesus Christ,
we sing your praise;
accept our music.
Lord Jesus Christ,
we dance your praise;
accept our movement.
Lord Jesus Christ,
we live your praise;
accept our souls and bodies.

## CHILDREN'S WORKSHOP

### Ice-breaker

Make a video recording of some different styles of dancing from the week's television, trying to include classic ballroom and modern disco dancing. Or provide appropriate music and invite the children to dance.

Discuss why people dance and how dance can express happiness, joy and celebration. Encourage them to talk about dancing in church as a way of giving thanks to God.

### Activities

- Provide several different types of music and invite the children to interpret the music in different forms of dance.
- Produce a collage (using magazine pictures and drawn pictures) of things for which we should thank God. Place at the centre of the collage the bread and wine of the eucharist.
- Make individual books or diaries of things for which the children wish to give thanks to God. Compose some prayers of thanks.

### Projects

- Learn and perform some country dances and dress up to dance them.
- Let the children work with a group of people who are used to liturgical dance.
- Develop the children's understanding of different forms of dancing. Discuss the different styles of dress associated with each and the different kinds of environment in which they generally take place. Produce collages of these different forms of dancing. Include, for example, music and movement in the school hall, country dancing in the old style barn, Scottish dancing by the loch side, morris dancing in the village market place, disco dancing in the church hall amid colourful lights, ballroom dancing in a grand ballroom.

### Discussion starters

- The children's experience of dancing
- Dance on television
- Ways of saying thank you to God
- Reasons for saying thank you to God

### Dance/drama

Prepare movement which can be shared to express thanks to God at the end of the communion service. This might involve disco dancing, country dancing or a gymnastic display.

# CELEBRATING TOGETHER

### All-age involvement

Invite all members of the congregation to think about the ways in which they expressed thanks at different stages of their lives, from infancy, through childhood and adolescence, into adulthood. Some may wish to illustrate these different phases by clipping pictures from magazines. Encourage them to discuss the different expressions of gratitude, and to recognise the value of the church providing opportunities for these different expressions.

### The service

When the members of the congregation have returned to their seats after receiving communion, invite them to think about the many different ways in which they can show their thanks to God for feeding them in the eucharist. Draw their attention to the activity work on dance and movement as one special way of saying thank you to God. If the children have prepared dance or a gymnastic display, this can be shared immediately after the post-communion prayer. Consider inviting a local dance group to prepare something for the service.

### Display

In the prayer after communion we thank God for feeding us in the eucharist. We offer to God our souls and bodies, our words and our dance.

# 30

# Rainbows

## KEY AIMS

- To help children and adults explore the Blessing
- To help the children explore the symbol of the rainbow
- To help the children appreciate the story of Noah as a sign of God's goodwill to his people
- To help the children experience the Blessing as God's goodwill to them

## WORSHIP RESOURCES

### Reference to communion service

*Blessing*

The Blessing is part of the Rite of Dismissal at the close of the communion service. In its biblical sense, blessing means primarily the active outgoing of God's goodwill, which results in prosperity and happiness among God's people. In biblical imagery, the dove, the olive branch and the rainbow are all signs of God's goodwill.

### Picture

The picture shows the rainbow filling the sky, while a dove flies past carrying an olive branch. Here are powerful images from the book of Genesis signalling the end of the great flood. The rainbow promises God's peace to the whole of creation.

### Bible story

*Signs of blessing given to Noah* (Genesis 8:10-11 and 9:14-16)

When the great flood came, Noah built an ark to save his family and all the animals. At last the waters began to go down. Then Noah sent a dove from the ark to see if anything was growing nearby. The dove returned with an olive branch in its beak and Noah knew that dry land was in sight. When the flood was over, God put a rainbow in the sky as a promise never to flood the earth like that again. God said to Noah, 'When I put clouds in the sky above the earth, the rainbow shall be seen in the clouds. Then I will remember my promise. Never again shall the waters become a flood to destroy all living creatures.' For this reason the rainbow still speaks to us of God's goodwill and blessing. May the blessing of God be among us and remain with us always!

## Hymns and songs

*Come and Praise*
Carpenter, carpenter, make me a tree (5)
Shalom, shalom, may peace be with you (141)
Who put the colours in the rainbow? (12)

*Hymns Ancient and Modern New Standard*
All people that on earth do dwell (100)
Lord Christ, the Father's mighty Son (386)
Sent forth by God's blessing (510)

*Hymns Old and New: New Anglican Edition*
May the grace of Christ our Saviour (333)
O Holy Ghost, thy people bless (370)
Who put the colours in the rainbow? (557)

*Complete Anglican Hymns Old and New*
God almighty set a rainbow (804)
God sends a rainbow after the rain (808)
There's a rainbow in the sky (893)

*Hymns and Songs for Assembly*
God made the colours of the rainbow (35)
Mister Noah built an ark (80)
Rise and shine and give God his glory (97)

## Bible readings

*Old Testament – Genesis 8:10-11 and 9:14-16
New Testament – Philippians 4:6-8
Gospel – John 14:23-27

## Prayer

Lord God,
you gave your servant Noah
the rainbow as a sign of blessing.
Bless us your servants today
with the gift of your peace
and the joy of your presence;
through Jesus Christ our Lord.

## CHILDREN'S WORKSHOP

### Ice-breaker

Find a picture of a rainbow. Encourage the children to talk about their experience of rainbows. Draw out their understanding of when they see rainbows and what causes them. If there is a science teacher in the local church, invite him or her to demonstrate with light and glass how light is refracted to produce the rainbow. Name the colours of the rainbow (red, orange, yellow, green, blue, indigo, violet). Then move directly to the story of the rainbow in the Scripture passage about Noah.

## Activities

- Make enough rainbow badges so that they can be distributed to all the children and adults attending the service. Cut the badges from white card; colour them in rainbow shadings; attach a safety pin to the back with strong tape.
- Make mobiles of the dove and olive branch to hang in the church. Suspend them from a rainbow.
- Produce an illustrated book telling the story of Noah's flood and reaching its climax in the rainbow and God's blessing.

## Projects

- Make a huge rainbow which can be displayed in church and perhaps be hoisted into position during the service. Make this from strong card. Glue on fabric or paper to show the rainbow colours.
- Listen to part of Benjamin Britten's *Noye's Fludde* and learn to sing or play short extracts.
- Create a large model of the ark, Noah's family and the animals, to stand in a corner of the church, or make costumes or head-dresses to represent Noah's family and the different animals.

## Discussion starters

- Pictures of rainbows
- Where the children have seen rainbows
- How the rainbow is used in myths, legends and stories
- Pictures of Noah's flood
- The dove and the olive branch

## Dance/drama

Produce a play or dance about the Noah story. Encourage the children to enter into the experience of being caught in a flood and waiting for the waters to go down. Then follows the experience of rescue and safety and God's promise that such a flood will never happen to them again.

# CELEBRATING TOGETHER

## All-age involvement

Invite the congregation to think about times in their lives when they have been aware of God's continuing favour. Provide pieces of coloured paper and pens for these experiences to be written down as a prayer: 'Thank you, God, for . . .' These prayers can be attached to a large rainbow in the church. Encourage people to talk together as they think and write.

## The service

Before the Blessing, invite the congregation to think about the relevance of the imagery of dove, olive branch and rainbow for the blessing. Introduce them to the activity work. If a huge rainbow has been prepared, this can now be hoisted into position. If rainbow badges have been made for the congregation, these can now be distributed and worn. If the children have made animal head-dresses, these can be put on and the children assembled under the rainbow. If the children have prepared dance or drama about the Noah story, this can be shared before the Blessing is pronounced.

## Display

The Blessing at the end of the communion service pronounces God's favour and goodwill. We are reminded of the covenant God made with Noah when God placed the rainbow in the sky.

# 31

# Helping hands

### KEY AIMS

- To help children and adults see ways they can serve Christ in his world
- To help the children identify need, deprivation and hardship in their own community
- To help the children be aware of the response made by members of the local church to the needs of their community
- To help the children appreciate the significance of the commission to love and serve the Lord

### WORSHIP RESOURCES

#### Reference to communion service

*Dismissal*

The Dismissal at the close of the communion service emphasises that worship leads on naturally to the Christian's daily life in the world. Worship is not something isolated from the rest of life, but something which determines the way in which the whole of life is lived. The Christian disciple is commissioned to go out into the world to love and serve the Lord.

#### Picture

The final picture shows the people back in the outside world. They have been sent out, to go in peace to love and serve the Lord in the world. This reminds us that everything which happens in church is a preparation for our Christian lives in the world.

#### Bible story

*Jesus sends the 12 disciples out in his name* (Mark 6:7-13, 30)

St Mark tells us how Jesus chose 12 people to be his special companions and disciples. For a long time these people followed Jesus everywhere he went. They listened carefully to what he said and watched closely what he did. Then Jesus sent these 12 disciples out in pairs to share his work and to do what he had been doing. When they came back they told Jesus all they had done and taught. At the end of the eucharist Jesus sends us out, just as he sent those 12 disciples, to carry on his work. Go in peace, therefore, to love and serve the Lord!

## Hymns and songs

*Come and Praise*
There's a child in the streets (27)
Would you walk by on the other side? (70)
You shall go out with joy (98)

*Hymns Ancient and Modern New Standard*
Forth in thy name, O Lord, I go (239)
Now let us from this table rise (403)
When I needed a neighbour, were you there? (433)

*Hymns Old and New: New Anglican Edition*
For I'm building a people of power (135)
From heav'n you came, helpless babe (148)
Go forth and tell (164)

*Complete Anglican Hymns Old and New*
Come on, let's get up and go (788)
Out into the great wide world we go (873)
There's a great big world out there (892)

*Hymns and Songs for Assembly*
I give my hands to do your work (48)
I, the Lord of sea and sky (59)
Love is something if you give it away (76)

## Bible readings

Old Testament – Deuteronomy 14:22, 28-29
New Testament – James 1:26-27
*Gospel – Mark 6:7-13, 30

## Prayer

Lord Jesus Christ,
send us out in your name,
to serve you by helping others.
Use our feet to run your errands;
use our hands to do your work;
use our eyes to show your love;
use our tongues to speak your words.
Lord Jesus Christ,
send us out in your name,
to your praise and glory.

## CHILDREN'S WORKSHOP

### Ice-breaker

Many of the well-known voluntary organisations, like the Red Cross, St John Ambulance, Women's Royal Voluntary Service and Rotary, have a distinctive logo or sign. Make pictures of some of these and ask the children what they stand for and what the organisations do. Broaden the discussion to include activities like meals on wheels, prison visiting, running Brownies and Cubs, etc. Discover which members of the congregation belong to these groups and invite them to attend the session. Divide the children into groups and suggest that the groups take it in turn to interview each of the adults about their voluntary work.

### Activities
- Make a poster or project book about the local voluntary organisations and the people from the church who contribute to their work. Use a title such as 'St Mark's church is active in the local community.'
- Make the logo and signs of caring organisations to hang in church as mobiles.
- Draw pictures of the ways you help others: at home, at school or in the wider community.

### Projects
- Discover how Jesus helped others in St Mark's Gospel and prepare a project book around these events, including, for example, healing Simon's mother-in-law (Mark 1:30-31), the leper (Mark 1:40-42), the paralysed man (Mark 2:6-12), the man with the withered arm (Mark 3:1-6), legion (Mark 5:1-17), Jairus' daughter (Mark 5:21-24, 35 43), the woman with haemorrhage (Mark 5:25-34), the deaf and dumb man (Mark 7:32-37), the blind man (Mark 8:22-26).
- Study one or two local voluntary organisations in depth – for example, the meals on wheels service. Discuss who organises it locally, the people who work for it, where the meals are cooked, how people benefit from the service, etc. Encourage the children to help with the local meals on wheels one day and to meet the people to whom the meals are taken.
- Work together to help people in need in your community. You could bake food or make objects for a stall to raise money, or you could give active help in a project such as gardening or cleaning for elderly people.

### Discussion starters
- People in need in the local community
- Local people who work in helping and caring professions
- Local voluntary organisations
- Jesus' ministry of helping and caring for others
- The helping and caring ministry of the 12 disciples

### Dance/drama
Develop a play about Jesus commissioning the 12 disciples and sending them out to carry on with his work of teaching and caring for others. Relate this to the needs of your local community.

## CELEBRATING TOGETHER

### All-age involvement

Invite the congregation to tell about the different places where they can serve the Lord – for example, home, school, work, shopping centres, playground, neighbours' homes, hospitals. Write each of these places on a separate sheet of poster paper. Separate into groups, each group to detail ways of serving Christ in one of these places.

### The service

After the post-communion prayer, invite the congregation to think about the way in which the communion service ends with them being sent out to love and serve the Lord in their daily lives. Draw attention to the activity work on helping hands. If drama has been prepared, it can be shared at this point. This would also be an opportunity for members of specific voluntary groups to talk to the whole congregation about the work of these groups. After this presentation, the service can close directly with the Dismissal, omitting the Blessing.

### Display

The communion service ends with the Dismissal. The Dismissal sends us out into the world and tells us to set our faith to work.

# Take-home sheets

## GETTING TO KNOW YOU

The communion service begins with the greeting
'The Lord be with you' and it means with each one of us.
This is a good time to get to know each other better.

## Prayer

All-loving God,
you know each one of us by name,
and you love us all.
Help us to feel your presence with us,
and to grow closer to each other;
through Jesus Christ our Lord.

## Bible story

### Jesus chooses 12 friends (Mark 3:13-19)

When Jesus began his work he chose 12 people to be his close friends. Jesus
wanted to get to know these friends very well; and he wanted them to learn about his
way of life by listening to what he said and watching what he did. Jesus' friends were
called Peter and Andrew, James and John, Philip, Bartholomew, Matthew, Thomas,
James, Thaddaeus, Simon and Judas. Jesus gave some of them nicknames, which
described the sort of people they were. Peter he called 'the Rock'; James and John he
called 'Sons of Thunder'. We, too, are called to be Jesus' close friends. He knows
each of us by name. 'The Lord be with you!'

## To do with others

### Questions and answers

How much do you really know about your family
likes and dislikes? How much does your family
really know about your likes and dislikes? Ask five
questions each to test it out. They can be questions
like 'Who's my favourite singer?' or 'What makes
me most angry?' Keep a record of the questions
and a score of total correct answers. Try the game
again three days later with the same questions.
See if the total family score has been improved.

> **Think about this**
> Who can you get
> to know better
> this week?

Name......................................................................................................................

Taken from *His Spirit is with us*, published by Kevin Mayhew.

# This is me

My name is

..........................................................

I was born on

..........................................................

This is what I look like. ⟶

My favourite colour is

..........................................................

My favourite food is

..........................................................

My favourite sports team is

..........................................................

These are my favourite activities. ⟶

**Paste on a photograph**

**Paste on pictures.**

What I like best about myself is

..........................................................................................................

**At the communion service we greet each other saying, 'The Lord be with you.'**
**It is a time to get to know each other better.**

Name...............................................................................................

Taken from *His Spirit is with us*, published by Kevin Mayhew.

# WAYS WITH WATER

The Collect for Purity is at the opening of the communion service.
Almighty God . . .
cleanse the thoughts of our hearts
by the inspiration of your Holy Spirit . . .
through Christ our Lord.
Amen.
It reminds us that we need God to prepare and cleanse us
before we come to worship. Each time we say this prayer we are reminded
of the water of our baptism.

## Prayer
Almighty God,
you make us clean
with the water of baptism
and accept us into your Church.
Send your Holy Spirit on us
to cleanse the thoughts of our hearts
and to make us ready to worship you;
through Jesus Christ our Lord.

## Bible story
### Philip baptises the Ethiopian official (Acts 8:26-40)
When people wanted to join the early disciples and apostles as members of the Church, they asked to be baptised. The Ethiopian official was someone like this. He had read about God in the Bible and Philip had told him the good news about Jesus. The Ethiopian official made up his mind that he wanted to join Jesus' followers. He said to Philip, 'Here is water: what is there to prevent my being baptised?' Philip asked him to speak aloud his faith in Jesus. He replied, 'I believe that Jesus Christ is the Son of God.' Philip led him down into the water and baptised him. He became a member of the Church. We, too, become members of the Church when we are baptised in water. We remember our baptism when we come to worship God in the eucharist and when we ask God to 'cleanse the thoughts of our hearts'.

## To do with others
### An information hunt
Have you been baptised? If so, when were you baptised? Who are your godparents? Do you have any certificates or photos of the event? Find out, with your family, about your baptism and that of each family member.

> **Think about this**
> When do you feel
> most clean?
> That's how
> you can feel after
> praying the
> Collect for Purity.

Name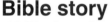.....

Taken from *His Spirit is with us*, published by Kevin Mayhew.

# Clean it up!

**Two experiments to try**

## 1. Dirty hands

Roll up your sleeves, cover your clothes and prepare for action!

First put out these cleansers:
- paper towels
- sand
- liquid soap
- clothes washing powder or liquid

and several bowls of water.

- a rag
- a bar of soap
- dishwashing detergent

Next find the dirtiest, greasiest mess your parents will let you touch. Cover your hands in dirt and try to clean it off. Use each cleanser in turn, dirtying your hands again after cleansing. Use each cleanser alone and then try it with water. Which is most effective? Record your results. Give each one a score from 0 to 10, 10 meaning completely clean.

## 2. A dirty rag

Find some old rags and smear them with dirt or oil. (Cooking oil will do.) Now wash each one separately in water and

- soap
- dishwashing detergent
- stain remover

- liquid soap
- clothes washing powder or liquid

| | CLEANSER | WITHOUT WATER | WITH WATER |
| :---: | :--- | :---: | :---: |
| **RECORD YOUR RESULTS** | Paper towels<br>Rag<br>Sand<br>Soap<br>Liquid soap<br>Detergent<br>Washing powder/liquid | **DIRTY HANDS** | DIRTY HANDS |
| | Soap<br>Liquid soap<br>Detergent<br>Washing powder/liquid<br>Stain remover | **DIRTY RAG** | DIRTY RAG |

**Before we come to worship we need God to cleanse us.**

Name......................................................................................................................

Taken from *His Spirit is with us*, published by Kevin Mayhew.

The Confession begins with the words:
  Most merciful God...
  we confess that we have sinned.
It invites us to examine the barriers we build between ourselves and other people and between ourselves and God. We are sorry about these barriers and ask God to forgive us.

## Prayer

Merciful God,
you sent your Son
to break down the barriers of sin.
Make us truly sorry for our misdeeds
and give us your pardon and peace,
that we may serve you
in newness of life;
through Jesus Christ our Lord.

## Bible story

### Jesus' summary of the law (Matthew 22:35-40)

In the Old Testament God gave Moses the Ten Commandments. The people were instructed to keep these laws and to base their lives on them. In the New Testament Jesus summed up all Ten Commandments as two key laws. Jesus said, 'Love the Lord your God with all your heart, with all your soul, with all your mind. That is the greatest commandment. It comes first. The second is like it. Love your neighbour as yourself.' When we break these great commandments we build up barriers between God and ourselves. That is why we need to confess our sins so that God may forgive us and remove the barriers.

## To do with others

### Build or break down a wall

Set aside part of your living room or hallway this week for construction. Place there a box full of building blocks (small Lego blocks will do). Every time someone in the family upsets another, putting a barrier between themselves, one person should place a block to build a wall. Every time someone in the family says sorry after hurting another, or does something particularly kind, a block can be removed. See if you can end the week without any part of a wall built.

> **Think about this**
> It is not easy to say sorry and mean it when you upset someone - but if you do not say sorry it can be like a high brick wall between the two of you.

Name....................................................................................................................

Taken from *His Spirit is with us*, published by Kevin Mayhew.

# Barriers of words

Sometimes the things we say can make barriers or walls between us and other people. Look at the statements below.

Which ones cut us off from people? Cut them out and glue them to the stones of the wall. Which ones bring us close to people? Cut them out and glue them to the bars of the gate.

I hate you

You're stupid

I'm sorry

I didn't mean it

I like you

I won't share

Get lost!

Can we start again?

Liar, liar, pants on fire!

Let's be friends

I'll help you

I won't be your friend any more

**At the Confession we think about the barriers we build between ourselves and other people and between ourselves and God. We ask God to forgive us.**

Name......................................................................................................................

Taken from *His Spirit is with us*, published by Kevin Mayhew.

The Absolution proclaims the forgiveness of sins. It says that the break in the relationship between us and God is mended, that there is no longer a barrier between us.

## Prayer

Forgiving God,
you give to your people
the freedom and joy of your forgiveness.
Help us freely to forgive others
as we have been freely forgiven;
through Jesus Christ our Lord.

## Bible story

### Forgiveness of sins (John 20:19-23)

On the first Easter Sunday evening, before they understood Jesus' resurrection, the disciples had met together and locked the door because they were afraid. Then Jesus came and stood there with them. 'Peace be with you!' he said. When the disciples saw the Lord they were filled with joy. Then Jesus commissioned them to carry on with his work. 'As the Father sent me,' he said, 'so I send you.' He breathed on them, saying, 'Receive the Holy Spirit! If you forgive anyone's sins, they are forgiven; if you pronounce them unforgiven, unforgiven they remain.' This passage from St John's Gospel is read when priests are ordained and the bishop passes on to them the authority to absolve sins in Christ's name. That is why the priest gives the absolution in the communion service and how we can be confident that our sins are forgiven.

## To do with others

### Plan a special event

When we are cross with each other we do not enjoy being together. Our family relationship is broken. When we say we are sorry and forgive each other then we mend the break in our relationship. Forgive each other; and celebrate by planning a special event together. It may be a special meal with someone's favourite food, all helping to prepare; it may be an outing to a park to feed the ducks or fly kites. Choose something you can all enjoy.

> **Think about this**
> Is there anything you have done that worries you? If you have asked God to forgive you, you can be sure God has done so.

Name.............................................................................................................................

Taken from *His Spirit is with us*, published by Kevin Mayhew.

# A repair record

We often need to repair objects or relationships. Keep a record of what you repair this week. If you repair any of those pictured below, write in the date and draw or write what you use to repair them – for example, tools, words, actions. If you repair any others, record them in the space provided and on your own paper.

*ripped book*

Date:
Repaired with:

*model*

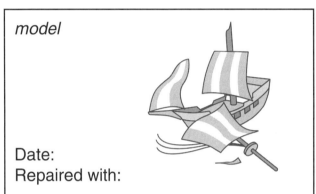

Date:
Repaired with:

*clothes*

Date:
Repaired with:

*friendship*

Date:
Repaired with:

*relationship with God*

Date:
Repaired with:

Date:
Repaired with:

**When God forgives us, the break in our relationship with God is repaired.**

Name..................................................................................................................

Taken from *His Spirit is with us*, published by Kevin Mayhew.

# MAKING MUSIC

The 'Glory to God' is a great Christian hymn of praise. It begins:
Glory to God in the highest,
and peace to his people on earth.
This comes from the angels' song at Bethlehem.
This song is praise to God our heavenly King, Lord Jesus Christ,
only Son of the Father and the Holy Spirit.
Music helps us to express the joy and happiness of our praise.

## Prayer
Lord God,
you give us an ear for music
and a heart for song.
Help us to praise you
with tambourines and dancing,
with recorders and singing,
with the clash of cymbals and the
fanfare of trumpets;
through Jesus Christ who lives in
harmony with you and the
Holy Spirit, now and for ever.

## Bible passage
*Praising God with the sound of music*
*(Psalm 150)*

Praise the Lord.
O praise God in his sanctuary:
praise him in the firmament of his power.

Praise him for his mighty acts:
praise him according to his abundant goodness.

Praise him in the blast of the ram's horn:
praise him upon the lute and harp.

Praise him with the timbrel and dances:
praise him upon the strings and pipe.

Praise him on the high sounding cymbals:
praise him on the loud cymbals.

Let everything that has breath praise the Lord:
O praise the Lord.
(*from the* **Good News Bible**)

## To do with others
*Play some music*
What music do you like to listen to?
What music do you like to work to?
What music makes you think about God?
Ask members of the family to talk about
the music they like to listen to and work to.
Then listen together to the music that
reminds each of you about God.

**Think about this**
What feelings do
you have when
you listen to
music? What
music makes you
feel you are
praising God?

Name......................................................................................................

Taken from *His Spirit is with us*, published by Kevin Mayhew.

# Make your own music

Read this hymn of praise and work out how to accompany it with an instrument.

Praise the Lord!

Praise God, sun and moon;
praise God, shining stars.
Praise God, highest heavens,
and the waters above the sky.

Praise the Lord from the earth,
sea-monsters and all ocean depths;
lightning and hail, snow and clouds,
strong winds that obey his command

Praise the Lord!
*(from Psalm 148 from the* **Good News Bible***)*

**Make your own melody instrument**
- Collect 8 glass bottles of the same size and shape.
- Mix some food colouring in a jug of water.
- Fill the first bottle full of water. Add slightly less to the next bottle and less again to the next and so on. Use a beater to tap your bottles and hear the sounds they make. Add water or pour it out until the bottles sound right, like the white notes on a piano. Experiment with your bottles until you find three that go well with the words 'Praise the Lord'.
- Try playing different bottles at the end of each line of your hymn of praise. (If you number your bottles you will be able to write down your choice for a friend to play.)

**Music helps us to express our joy and happiness when we praise God.**

Name........................................................................................................................

Taken from *His Spirit is with us*, published by Kevin Mayhew.

## YOUR CLERGY

When the president says the Collect, this prayer is offered on behalf of the whole congregation. The Collect makes us think of the clergy's special job in the church.

## Prayer

Almighty God,
you call deacons and priests
to your service.
Strengthen those whom you have called
that they may faithfully serve you,
to the glory of your name
and to the benefit of your Church;
through Jesus Christ, our great High Priest.

## When priests are ordained

Many things happen before priests are ordained. They go away to a selection conference where they are carefully interviewed to see how suitable they are to be priests. They are selected for training. They go on a training course to study, to gain skills, and to grow in prayer. At last they are ordained, probably in a cathedral. You can read the ordination service in the modern prayer book.

**Think about this**
You are an important part of your church. When the priest or deacon says the Collect, they are praying on your behalf.

## To do with others
*Make a list*
You see your vicar in the Sunday services but what about the rest of the week? Think back over the past year. Where else have you seen your vicar? What else do you know that your vicar does in the church?

Name............................................................................................................

Taken from *His Spirit is with us*, published by Kevin Mayhew.

# Design a stole

Some deacons and priests wear stoles with special designs embroidered on them. These designs could be a special Christian symbol; they could reflect a special interest of the priest or deacon; or they could reflect the history of the Church.

Design a stole particularly suited to your own church.

**The designs on the stole remind us of the work of the priest.**

Name.............................................................................................................

Taken from *His Spirit is with us*, published by Kevin Mayhew.

The Bible is a rich library of books. It includes history, poetry, prophecy, letters, and gospels. In the Ministry of the Word God speaks to people today through the Bible.

## Prayer

Blessed Lord,
you have given the Bible to your people.
Help us to hear your word,
that we may know you clearly,
love you deeply
and serve you fully;
through Jesus Christ, your living Word.

## Bible story

### Jesus reads from the Bible in Nazareth (Luke 4:14-21)

Jesus used to go to the synagogue on the Sabbath day. Sometimes he was asked to read from the Bible and to interpret the reading in an address. In those days the Bible was not printed like the books we know today. Printing had not been invented. Instead the Bibles were written out by hand on long scrolls. One day when Jesus was visiting his home town of Nazareth they asked him to read the lesson and handed him the scroll of the prophet Isaiah. He opened the scroll and read the passage which says 'The Spirit of the Lord is upon me because he has anointed me.' Then he rolled up the scroll, gave it back to the attendant and sat down to teach. 'Today,' he said, 'in your very hearing this text has come true.' In the same way every Sunday we listen to the words of the Bible read in church and the preacher helps us to understand what those words mean for us today. 'This is the word of the Lord: thanks be to God.'

## To do with others

### Learn a Bible passage

Many people learn to say parts of the Bible from memory. Choose a short passage and see if your family can learn to say it together. You could choose part of a psalm or part of Jesus' teachings like Matthew 5:43-48.

> **Think about this**
> God still speaks to us through the Bible. What Bible passages mean a lot to you?

Name...........................................................................................

Taken from *His Spirit is with us*, published by Kevin Mayhew.

# A memory game

1. Cut the squares below into 16 cards. (If you want this game to last you could glue the page onto cardboard before cutting.)
2. Shuffle your cards and lay them out face down.
3. With one or more friends, take turns to turn two cards over. If your cards match, you keep the pair and have another turn. If the cards do not match, the next player has a turn. Keep playing until all the cards are paired. For the cards to match, the words will not be the same but they will be the same type of book – for example, two history cards.

| | | | |
|---|---|---|---|
| **HISTORY** Solomon was king of all Israel. **1 KINGS 4:1** | **HISTORY** The people of Israel were divided: some of them wanted to make Tibni son of Ginarth king. **1 KINGS 16:21** | **POETRY & SONG** O Lord, our Lord, your greatness is seen in all the world! **PSALM 8:1** | **POETRY & SONG** Praise him with cymbals. Praise him with loud cymbals. **PSALM 150:5** |
| **WISDOM** Sensible people accept good advice. People who talk foolishly will come to ruin. **PROVERBS 10:8** | **WISDOM** Kind words bring life, but cruel words crush your spirit. **PROVERBS 15:4** | **PROPHECY** All the cities of Israel will be destroyed. **EZEKIEL 6:6** | **PROPHECY** I will gather them out of the countries where I scattered them, and will give the land of Israel back to them. **EZEKIEL 11:17** |
| **LETTERS** From Paul . . . to God's people in Ephesus. **EPHESIANS 1:1** | **LETTERS** From Paul and Timothy, servants of Christ Jesus – To all God's people in Philippi. **PHILIPPIANS 1:1** | **LETTERS** With my own hands I write this: Greetings from Paul. **COLOSSIANS 4:18** | **LETTERS** And so I write to all of you in Rome whom God loves and has called to be his own people. **ROMANS 1:7** |
| **GOSPELS** This is the Good News about Jesus Christ, the Son of God. **MARK 1:1** | **GOSPELS** Jesus went all over Galilee, teaching in the synagogues, preaching the Good News. **MATTHEW 4:23** | **LAW** Do not spread false rumours. **EXODUS 23:1** | **LAW** Do not ill-treat a foreigner. **EXODUS 23:9** |

**Remember, the Bible is a library of books of different types. God still speaks to people through the Bible.**

Name..................................................................................................................

Taken from *His Spirit is with us*, published by Kevin Mayhew.

# FOLLOW THE SIGNS

We use signs and images to talk about God. God is like a parent who loves us, a shepherd who cares for us, a vine dresser who shapes us, a rock who protects us.

## Prayer

Dear Lord God,
you are a mighty rock,
protect us.
You are a shepherd,
care for us.
You are a vine dresser,
shape us.
You are a king,
rule over us.
You are a guardian,
love us.
You are a still small voice,
speak to us.
We make our prayer
in the name of Jesus Christ our Lord.

## Bible story

### *The burning bush* (Exodus 3:1-6)

Moses was out in the wilderness, looking after the sheep of his father-in-law, Jethro. God had chosen Moses for the special task of leading his people to a new country. While he was minding the sheep, Moses saw a burning bush. Although the bush was on fire, it was not being burnt up. When Moses turned aside to look at the bush, God spoke to him out of the bush and called him by name, 'Moses, Moses.' And Moses answered, 'I am here.' Through the burning bush Moses heard the voice of God.

## To do with others

### *A riddle game*

How is God like a caring parent? *(God loves us.)*
How is God like McDonald's? *(God is known all over the world.)*
How is God like a potter? *(God moulds us to shape.)*
Make up your own riddles using modern images of God.
Try them out with your family and friends.

> **Think about this**
> Which picture of God means most to you? How do you like to think about God?

Name..................................................................................................................

Taken from *His Spirit is with us*, published by Kevin Mayhew.

# Have you ever lost your voice?

When you cannot talk for a while you use signs to communicate. Some people cannot talk or hear at all. British Sign Language is one way of helping these people to communicate. Practise these signs. Try them out with a friend. If you enjoy them you could find more in your local library.

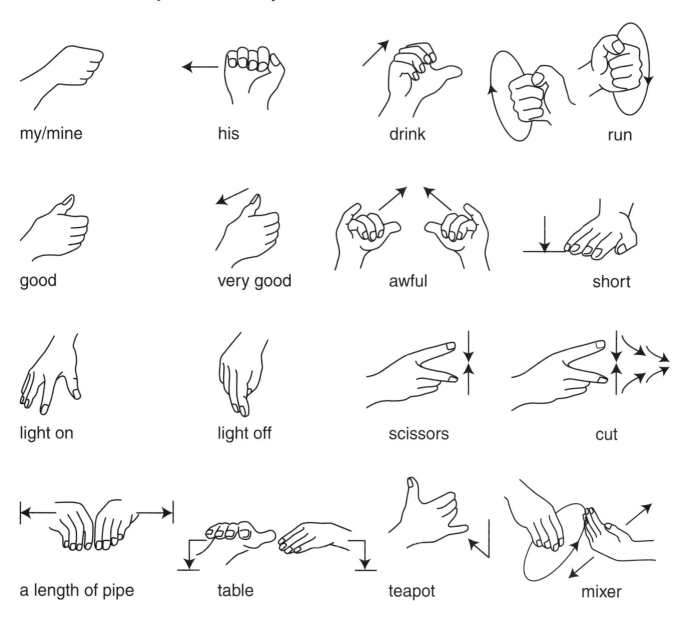

my/mine

his

drink

run

good

very good

awful

short

light on

light off

scissors

cut

a length of pipe

table

teapot

mixer

**It is hard to talk about God in ways we can understand.
That is why the Bible uses signs and images to describe God as a parent who loves us or a shepherd who cares for us.**

Name..................................................................................

Taken from *His Spirit is with us*, published by Kevin Mayhew.

# MEETING JESUS OF NAZARETH

Jesus was born in Palestine about 2000 years ago. He was crucified and rose from the dead. We believe Jesus is the Son of God.

## Prayer

God our guide,
you led the shepherds to see the infant Jesus;
you led the disciples to see the risen Lord.
Lead us to know his presence with us,
that we may share his risen life.
He lives and reigns
with you and the Holy Spirit,
now and always.

## Bible events about Jesus

You know a lot of stories about Jesus. Do you know the order in which they are written in the Bible? Here are some stories, all taken from the Gospel of Luke, written in order.

Jesus' birth (Luke 2:1-20)
Jesus at age 12 in Jerusalem (Luke 2:41-52)
Jesus called some disciples (Luke 5:1-11)
Jesus healed a paralysed man (Luke 5:17-26)
Jesus was helped by some women (Luke 8:1-3)
Jesus calmed a storm (Luke 8:22-25)
Jesus healed Jairus' daughter (Luke 8:40-42, 49-56)
Jesus told stories about a lost sheep, coin, and son (Luke 15:1-32)
Jesus met Zacchaeus (Luke 19:1-10)
Jesus was angry in the temple (Luke 19:45-46)
Jesus ate a last supper with the disciples (Luke 22:14-23)
Jesus was arrested (Luke 22:47-54)
Jesus was crucified and buried (Luke 23:26-56)
Jesus rose to new life (Luke 24:1-12)
Jesus ascended to heaven (Luke 24:50-53)

> **Think about this**
> Which story about Jesus do you most enjoy? What does this story tell you about Jesus?

## To do with others

### A word search

Together work out words to describe Jesus. You could try to find one word for each letter of the alphabet (for example, Active, Brave, Capable). If your time is short you could work individually or in pairs to find adjectives for each letter of 'Jesus', then read your words to each other.

Name.............................................................................................................

Taken from *His Spirit is with us*, published by Kevin Mayhew.

# What is Jesus like?

Bible stories tell us in words what Jesus did and what he is like. For some ideas, read Matthew 8:1-3, Mark 8:1-10, Luke 18:15-17, and John 6:16-21.

Artists use pictures to show us what they think Jesus is like. By the expression in his face they show the sort of person they think he is from their reading of the Bible stories. Look at these pictures. Which one is closest to the way you imagine Jesus to be?

1.

2.

3.

4. *Draw your own picture of Jesus.*

**The more we learn about Jesus, the more we can love him.**

Name.................................................................................................................

Taken from *His Spirit is with us*, published by Kevin Mayhew.

## WINDY DAY

The image which tells us most about God the Holy Spirit is the picture of the wind. We cannot see the wind and yet we know that it is there, all around us.

## Prayer

Almighty God,
you sent your Holy Spirit
like the wind from heaven,
to strengthen the disciples.
Fill us with the same Spirit
that we may share in their work;
through Jesus Christ our Lord.

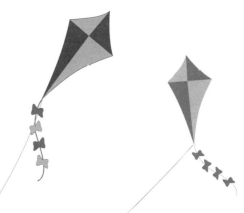

## Bible story
### Day of Pentecost (Acts 2:1-4)

After Jesus rose from the dead on Easter Sunday he appeared to his disciples and taught them about the kingdom of God over a period of 40 days. He promised them that he would send the Holy Spirit to them. On the day of Pentecost all the disciples were together in the same place. Suddenly there came from the sky a noise like a strong driving wind which filled the whole house where they were sitting. And there appeared to them tongues like flames of fire, which rested on each of them. And they were all filled with the Holy Spirit. The Holy Spirit gave them new power to proclaim the good news about Jesus and the resurrection.

## To do with others
### Fly a kite

Get out together and fly a kite or a paper aeroplane. Watch leaves drifting in the wind. Talk about times you have been out in the wind, in a gentle breeze or a howling gale. Which most reminds you of the work of the Holy Spirit?

**Think about this**
When you fly paper aeroplanes you can sometimes improve their flight by changing their shapes. What can you do so that the Holy Spirit can better work through you?

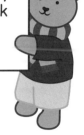

Name.................................................................................................................

Taken from *His Spirit is with us*, published by Kevin Mayhew.

# Fly a whirly-wing

## Instructions

1. Cut out the whirly-wing on the heavy black lines.
2. Fold the beak under on the dotted lines.

3. Fold the beak back.

4. Fold one wing forward and one wing back.

5. Hold the whirly-wing up high (perhaps at an upstairs window) and drop it. Watch it spin and whirl.

## Experiment

What happens if you cut out a beak shape instead of folding back paper?

What happens if you add a paper clip to the beak?

What happens if you do not fold one wing forward?

**We cannot see the wind but we can see how it makes the whirly-wing soar. The wind is an image used for God the Holy Spirit.**

Name..................................................................

Taken from *His Spirit is with us*, published by Kevin Mayhew.

# BETWEEN FRIENDS

The prayer for the Church and for the world reminds us that we should talk with God about everything that is important to us. At the same time, we should share in God's concerns for the world.

## Prayer

Almighty God,
you take an interest in all we do
and listen to what we have to say.
Help us to hear your word
that we may learn to pray
the prayers you desire from us;
through Jesus Christ our Lord.

## Bible story

### Jesus spends time in prayer (Mark 1:32-38)

St Mark's Gospel shows that Jesus often lived a very busy and very full life. People crowded around him to hear his teaching and to be healed by him. One evening it seemed as if the whole town was gathered around the house where he was staying. Even after sunset they kept bringing to him all who were ill or possessed by devils. He healed many and drove out many devils. Very early next morning Jesus got up and went out alone. He went away to a lonely spot and stayed there in prayer. These occasions of quiet and prayer were very important to Jesus as times when he could share his life with God the Father. We, too, need time to share with God, to tell God what we have been doing and to listen carefully to what God wants of us.

## To do with others

### Make a prayer box

Cover a box to look attractive. Perhaps you could use pictures of beautiful scenery to remind you to thank God for the beautiful world we have been given. Leave paper and pens next to the box. Invite family and friends to write out prayers and place them in the box for others to read, or to write down matters that concern them and leave these in the box for others to pray about.

> **Think about this**
> What is some news you would like to tell your best friend? God likes hearing news like this too.

Name.................................................................................................................

Taken from *His Spirit is with us*, published by Kevin Mayhew.

# My prayer diary

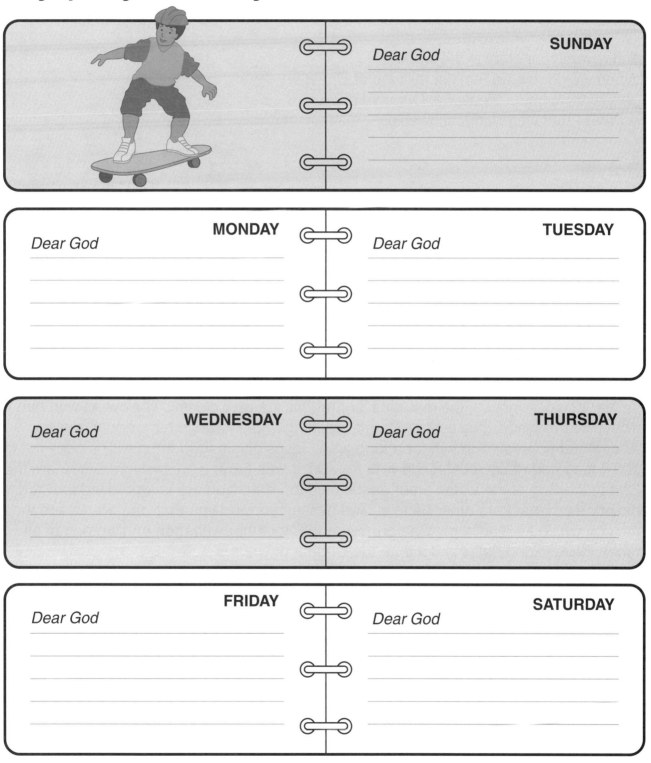

**SUNDAY**

*Dear God*

**MONDAY**

*Dear God*

**TUESDAY**

*Dear God*

**WEDNESDAY**

*Dear God*

**THURSDAY**

*Dear God*

**FRIDAY**

*Dear God*

**SATURDAY**

*Dear God*

**We can talk with God about everything that is important to us.**

Name.....................................................................................................

Taken from *His Spirit is with us*, published by Kevin Mayhew.

We pray for the Church, asking
that those who confess your name
may be united in your truth,
live together in your love,
and reveal your glory in the world.
When we do this we think of millions of Christian
people throughout the world. Our own church
is part of that worldwide fellowship.

## Prayer

Almighty God,
you call people of all races
into membership of your Church.
Hear our prayer for your people,
that all may serve you faithfully
to the glory of your holy name;
through our Lord and Saviour Jesus Christ.

## Bible story

### Jesus builds his Church (Matthew 16:13-19)

Jesus' 12 close friends, the disciples, shared his life very closely. They went with him
from place to place; they listened to his teaching and shared in his work of healing.
After they had been with him for a long time, Jesus challenged them with a question to
see if they had really recognised who he was. It was Peter who answered, 'You are the
Christ, the Son of the Living God!' Jesus said to Peter, 'You are favoured indeed! You
did not learn that from other people. God himself showed you that. You, Peter, are the
rock on which I will build my Church.' You and I, together with men and women of all
races, have joined Peter to become the Church of Christ.

## To do with others

### Complete a map

Display a map of the world. Think of friends
and relations or famous people who live
in other countries. Write out their names
and place them on the edges of the map,
with coloured wool or cotton joining the names
to the places where they live. Put a sign above
saying 'God's Church is everywhere!' You
could pray for these people by name.

> **Think about this**
> You pray for people in
> other countries. They
> pray for you. That is
> what it means to be
> part of God's
> worldwide church.

Name.................................................................................................................

Taken from *His Spirit is with us*, published by Kevin Mayhew.

# Pray for your church

- Make seven church cards like the ones below.
- Write a different name on each card. Choose people from your local church or choose different churches in your area or in the world.
- Put the cards in a bag. Each day choose a card from the bag and pray for that person or church.

## You will need

coloured card    scissors
glue    pens

## What to do

1.    Fold a square of coloured card in half.

2.    Cut out the shape of a church from card of a different colour. Draw the details of the church with pen.

3.    Glue the church shape on the front of the folded card.

4.    Inside the card write the name of a person or church.

St Michael's Church
Great Deeping

**The Church is made up of people just like you.
God's Church is spread throughout the whole world.**

Name.........................................................................................................

Taken from *His Spirit is with us*, published by Kevin Mayhew.

## AROUND THE WORLD

When we pray for the world we think of all that God created and everyone for whom Christ died. We need to share in God's care and love for the peoples of the world.

## Prayer

Almighty God,
you created the world
and intended all people to live in unity.
Where there is war, bring peace;
where there is hatred, bring love;
where there is anger, bring forgiveness;
for the sake of Jesus Christ,
your Son, our Lord.

## Bible story

### The many languages of the world (Genesis 11:1-9 and Acts 2:5-11)

Once upon a time, all the world spoke a single language and used the same words. 'Come,' they said, 'let us build ourselves a city and a tower with its top in the heavens, and make a name for ourselves.' So they made bricks, baked them hard and built tall. God was angry with what they had done and said, 'Here they are, one people with a single language, and now they have started to do this; now nothing they have a mind to do will be beyond their reach.' So God scattered them from that place and made a confusion of their speech, so that they could not understand what they said to each other. That place became known as Babel, because God made a babble of the languages of the world. Now God wants you and me and the whole of the Church to work on healing those divisions.

## To do with others

### An alphabetical race

Find the names of countries or cities for as many letters of the alphabet as you can. Use an atlas to help you. You could work in two teams, racing against each other to see who is fastest and who can find names for more letters of the alphabet. Display your lists. Pray for these places during the week.

**Think about this**
God loves you;
God loves the
rest of the world
too. What can you
do to share or
show that love?

Name...............................................................................................

Taken from *His Spirit is with us*, published by Kevin Mayhew.

# Pray for God's world

God has given us a responsibility for this world. As well as looking after our own part of it, we can pray for the rest of it. We can pray for wisdom for the world's leaders. We can pray for people who are suffering. We can rejoice with those people for whom life is going well.

Make your own prayer book. Staple sheets of paper together as a book. On the cover put a heading such as 'Prayers for God's world'.

Look through newspapers and magazines for pictures and headings about our world. Cut these out and paste them into your book. Include information about disasters such as famine, floods, war, illness and earthquakes. Also include pictures of beautiful scenery and of people loving and helping each other, to remind you to praise and thank God.

When you use a newspaper or magazine article, find out which country it is from and colour in that country on the map of the world below. You could glue this world map to the front cover of your book. Use your book to help you pray.

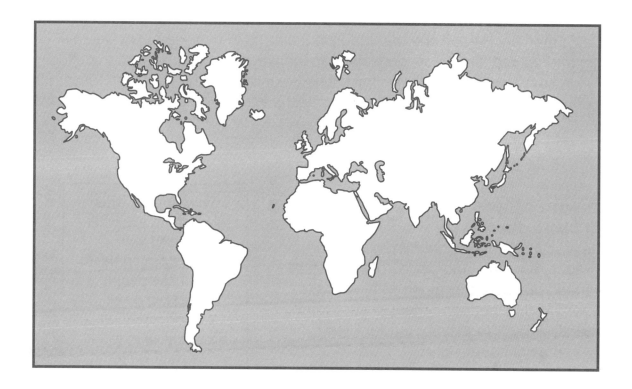

**Each day we can ask God's help for our world.**

Name...................................................................................................................

Taken from *His Spirit is with us*, published by Kevin Mayhew.

# MEET THE NEIGHBOURS

When we pray for our neighbourhood, we think of our family, our friends, and all the people who live and work in our area.

## Prayer

Loving God,
you teach us to love all people as our neighbours
and to love our neighbours as ourselves.
Make us alert to the needs of those around us
and help us to be of service to them;
through Jesus Christ our Lord.

## Bible story

### The Good Samaritan (Luke 10:29-37)

A teacher of the law asked Jesus the question, 'Who is my neighbour?' Jesus told this story in reply. A man was travelling along the road from Jerusalem to Jericho. Robbers attacked him, stripped him, beat him and went off leaving him half dead. A priest on his way to the temple in Jerusalem came along. He saw the man and went by on the other side. So did a Levite who was also on his way to the temple. Then a foreigner came along, a Samaritan. He saw the man and went across to him. He bandaged his wounds, and carried him on his donkey to an inn where he paid for him to be looked after. 'Now,' said Jesus, 'who do you think was neighbour to the man who fell into the hands of robbers?' Yes, the Samaritan. Now Jesus wants you and me to be like that Samaritan.

## To do with others

### Make a photo display

Together, walk around your community taking photographs of people and places of interest. Mount these photographs, along with others of your family, on a board or sheet of cardboard. Underneath write, 'We pray for our families, friends, and neighbours.'

---

**Think about this**
Next time you walk around your neighbourhood, look at all the people. These are the people for whom you pray each week in the liturgy.

---

Name..............................................................................................................

Taken from *His Spirit is with us*, published by Kevin Mayhew.

# A neighbourhood puzzle

Find the 28 hidden words in the puzzle below. (The words go forwards, backwards, up, down, and diagonally.) Mark the words in the puzzle with a line through them. Copy out the left-over letters to read what we pray for these people.

| W | C | T | E | P | E | C | I | L | O | P | R | A | Y | T |
| O | H | S | S | E | R | R | V | E | G | C | H | M | R | N |
| N | E | I | G | H | B | O | U | R | S | R | I | U | A | P |
| A | M | T | S | R | U | S | R | E | E | T | O | M | S | A |
| M | I | N | I | O | T | S | E | K | G | N | T | C | R | P |
| K | S | E | O | T | C | I | S | A | D | S | N | E | E | E |
| L | T | D | N | C | H | N | S | B | U | A | E | N | P | R |
| I | E | O | A | O | E | G | E | D | J | T | L | V | E | B |
| M | A | H | M | D | R | P | R | E | R | A | C | I | E | O |
| N | C | D | E | L | Y | A | D | O | V | E | N | C | W | Y |
| A | H | S | R | L | H | T | R | E | T | N | U | A | S | L |
| O | E | D | I | S | T | R | I | C | T | N | U | R | S | E |
| V | R | M | F | E | S | O | A | B | R | O | T | H | E | R |
| U | A | S | X | X | X | L | H | S | D | N | E | I | R | F |
| F | S | H | O | P | A | S | S | I | S | T | A | N | T | X |

## Word-list

| AUNT | BAKER | BROTHER | BUTCHER |
| CHEMIST | CROSSING PATROL | DAD | DENTIST |
| DISTRICT NURSE | DOCTOR | DUSTMAN | FAMILY |
| FIREMAN | FRIENDS | GROCER | HAIRDRESSER |
| JUDGE | ME | MILKMAN | MUM |
| NEIGHBOURS | PAPERBOY | POLICE | SHOP ASSISTANT |
| SWEEPERS | TEACHER | UNCLE | VICAR |

**When we pray for our neighbourhood we think of all these people and many more.**

Name.................................................................................

Taken from *His Spirit is with us*, published by Kevin Mayhew.

When we pray for the suffering, we think of all who are sick in body, mind or spirit. We also pray for those concerned with the healing and helping professions.

## A prayer

Almighty God,
your Son Jesus Christ healed the sick
and brought them to wholeness of life.
Where there is pain, bring healing;
where there is sickness, bring health;
where there is unhappiness, bring hope;
that all may share Christ's risen life,
who reigns with you and the Holy Spirit,
now and for ever.

## A bible story

### Jesus heals a paralysed man (Mark 2:1-12)

When Jesus came back to Capernaum, news quickly got around about where he was staying. Such a crowd gathered that the door to the house was blocked. Then four men came carrying their paralysed friend on a stretcher in the hope that Jesus would cure him. When they saw that they could not get in through the door, they went up to the flat roof of the house. They broke through the roof covering and lowered their friend down on the stretcher. Jesus saw their faith and said to the paralysed man, 'My son, your sins are forgiven. Stand up, take your bed, and go home.' The man got up, took his stretcher and went out in full view of everyone there. They were amazed and said, 'Never before have we seen anything like this.' Jesus continues to care for the sick and wants us to bring them to him in our prayers, just as those four men brought their friend on the stretcher.

## To do with others

### Visit or phone

Make a visit with family or friends to someone who is unwell or housebound. Ask if they would like you to do some shopping or gardening or housework. If you know someone who is too ill for visits, or lives too far away, phone or send a letter. If you do not know anyone who is ill, ask your vicar for the name of someone who is housebound and may need help.

> **Think about this**
> What was the worst thing about the last time you were unwell? You can pray for others who are feeling like that.

Name..................................................................................................

Taken from *His Spirit is with us*, published by Kevin Mayhew.

# A game to play

| Dental Emergency | Dental help | Medical Emergency | | | Medical help | Dental help |
| --- | --- | --- | --- | --- | --- | --- |
| Medical help | | | | | Medical help | |
| | | | | | Dental Emergency | |
| Medical Emergency | | | | | | |
| Dental help | | | | | Dental help | |

**Instructions**

1. Each player puts a button or counter on **START.**
2. Set a time limit for your game, perhaps 20 minutes.
3. In turn, throw a dice to see how many blocks to move.
4. Any player landing on a **Medical Emergency** block must remain there, missing turns, until another player lands on a *Medical Help* block and agrees to give up his or her next turn. The stuck player can then continue. If two players are on emergency blocks, the player on the help block must choose which one to help.
5. Any player landing on a **Dental Emergency** block must similarly remain until another player lands on a *Dental Help* block and agrees to help.
6. If a player lands on a *Help* block but no other player needs help, play continues.
7. Keep track of the number of times you help another player. The winner at the end of the chosen time is the player who has helped the most number of times.

| | Medical help | Medical Emergency | Dental help | Dental Emergency | Medical help | START |
| --- | --- | --- | --- | --- | --- | --- |

**When we pray for the suffering we think of all who are ill and all who help them.**

Name..............................................................................................

Taken from *His Spirit is with us*, published by Kevin Mayhew.

## LIGHT AND LIFE

In the eucharist the whole Church of Christ, living and departed, is united. We share our celebration with all the saints.

## Prayer

Almighty God,
you have called people to your service in every age.
Help us to follow in the footsteps of your saints,
that we may share with them Christ's risen life,
who reigns with you and the Holy Spirit,
now and for ever.

## Bible story

### Called to be saints (Matthew 5:1-12)

The word *saint* means *holy*. The saints of God are holy people. They are not people who lived a long time ago and in far-off places. They are not people who wear haloes on their heads and smile out from stained glass windows. They are people who have responded to God's call to live holy lives in God's service. In Matthew's Gospel, Jesus paints a picture of those who are called to be saints. He says:

Happy are those who know their need of God.
Happy are those who are sorrowful for their sins.
Happy are those who live gentle lives.
Happy are those who hunger and thirst to see right done.
Happy are those who show mercy to others.
Happy are those who have pure hearts.
Happy are those who make peace.
Happy are those who suffer persecution because they stand for what is right.

Jesus speaks these words to you and me. We are called to be saints.

## To do with others

### Visit a graveyard

Walk together around a graveyard. If you have any friends or relatives buried there, visit their graves. Look at the tombstones and read the inscriptions. Take note of one or two names so you can especially think of these people each week during the prayer for the departed.

**Think about this**
The saints were people who loved God and others. You too can live like a saint.

Name.................................................................................

Taken from *His Spirit is with us*, published by Kevin Mayhew.

# A saint's calendar

The Church remembers the early apostles on special days of the year, as lights to the Church. The Church associates a special emblem with each of the apostles. The emblems depict stories from the Bible or from what we think happened to these men. Colour in the emblems below. Read why each apostle was given his emblem. Cut them out and paste them on a calendar so you can remember each apostle on his special day.

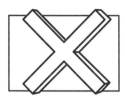

**St Andrew** - 30 November
*(silver cross, blue background)*
Andrew is said to have been crucified on this shape cross.

**St Matthew** - 21 September
*(silver money bags, red background)*
Matthew used to be a tax collector.

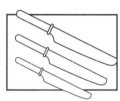

**St Bartholomew** - 24 August
*(silver knives with gold handles, red background)*
Bartholomew is said to have been flayed.

**St Matthias** - 24 February
*(open book and silver axe, red background)*
Matthias is said to have been beheaded.

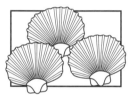

**St James the Great** - 25 July
*(gold shells, blue background)*
The shells are said to refer to pilgrimage.

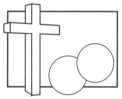

**St Philip** - 1 May
*(gold cross, silver circles, red background)*
The circles represent the two loaves Philip brought to Jesus to feed the five thousand.

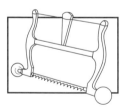

**St James the Less** - 1 May
*(silver saw with gold handle, red background)*
James is said to have been sawn in two.

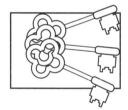

**St Peter** - 29 June
*(silver keys, red background)*
The keys represent the keys of the kingdom of heaven given to Peter.

**St John** - 27 December
*(gold cup, silver serpent, blue background)*
John is said to have been offered a poisoned cup to drink.

**St Simon** - 28 October
*(gold book, silver fish, red background)*
Simon was a fisher of people.

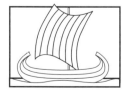

**St Jude** - 28 October
*(gold ship with silver sails, red background)*
Jude is said to have travelled to many places.

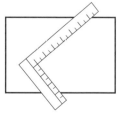

**St Thomas** - 21 December
*(carpenter's square with silver blade and gold handle, red background)*
Thomas is said to have built a church in East India.

**We are called to be lights to our world.**

Name...........................................................................................................

Taken from *His Spirit is with us*, published by Kevin Mayhew.

## SAY IT WITH HANDS

At the Peace we say:

The peace of the Lord be always with you
**and also with you.**

We say that we mean to accept and welcome each other as followers of Christ.
The outward sign of that is the hand clasp.

## Prayer

Almighty God,
your Son proclaimed peace to his followers.
Give us your peace in our lives
that we may learn
to forgive with hope,
to share with joy
and to serve with love.
We make our prayer
in the name of the Prince of Peace.

## Bible story

### Jesus tells us to make peace (Matthew 5:9, 23-24)

St Matthew tells us how Jesus taught his disciples and the crowds in his famous
Sermon on the Mount. One of the things Jesus said was this: 'How happy are the
people who make peace. God shall call them his sons and daughters.' Then Jesus
went on to explain how much God values people who make peace. He said, 'If you are
bringing your gift to God's altar and suddenly remember that you are angry with
someone, leave your gift where it is. First go and make peace with that person and
then come back and offer your gift.' That is why we share the Peace in church before
offering our gifts to God on the altar.

## To do with others

### Shape your hands

Think about the different things our hands
can do and what they tell us. Use your
hands to make shapes that show these
things. Show helping hands, tired hands,
angry hands, resting hands, hands of
praise, hands of punishment. Finish with
hands of greeting and welcome.

**Think about this**
At church we accept
and welcome each
other with a
hand clasp.
How do you show your
acceptance of others
at school?

Name.......................................................................................................................

Taken from *His Spirit is with us*, published by Kevin Mayhew.

# Our hands remind us

At church we greet each other with a hand clasp as a sign of peace. This peacemaking needs to take place all week. Choose six people to focus on this week. Let your hands help you to remember. Look at the description below of some parts of the hand. Choose one person for each description. Write their names on the picture of the hand. Every time you use your hand, let it remind you to share peace with these people.

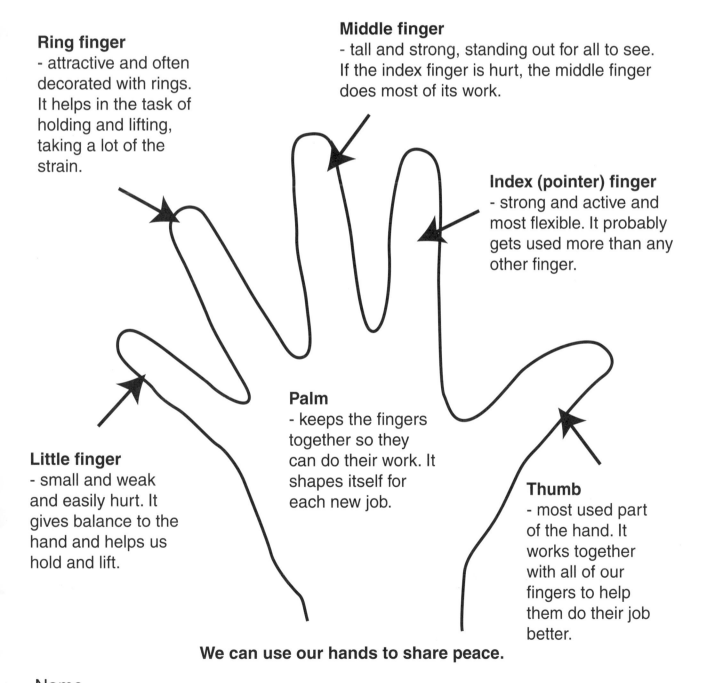

**Ring finger**
- attractive and often decorated with rings. It helps in the task of holding and lifting, taking a lot of the strain.

**Middle finger**
- tall and strong, standing out for all to see. If the index finger is hurt, the middle finger does most of its work.

**Index (pointer) finger**
- strong and active and most flexible. It probably gets used more than any other finger.

**Little finger**
- small and weak and easily hurt. It gives balance to the hand and helps us hold and lift.

**Palm**
- keeps the fingers together so they can do their work. It shapes itself for each new job.

**Thumb**
- most used part of the hand. It works together with all of our fingers to help them do their job better.

**We can use our hands to share peace.**

Name...................................................................................................................

Taken from *His Spirit is with us*, published by Kevin Mayhew.

# SHOPPING SPREE

At the preparation of the gifts we bring bread and wine to the altar as symbols of all the fruits of the earth and of all the work of human hands.

## Prayer

Almighty God,
all things come from you.
We praise you for your goodness.
Help us to use your gifts properly,
for our own well-being,
for the help of those in need
and for your glory;
through Jesus Christ our Lord.

## Bible story

### *King David praises God* (1 Chronicles 29:10-13)

King David decided to build a grand temple for God in the city of Jerusalem. He gave a lot of his own wealth towards the temple and invited other people to do the same. Many people gave very generously. When King David dedicated all their gifts to God he composed this great hymn of praise:

Blessed are you, Lord God of Israel.
Yours, Lord, is the greatness,
the power, the glory, the splendour, and the majesty;
for everything in heaven and on earth is yours.

We remember King David's words when we bring gifts of bread and wine to the altar.

## To do with others

### *Grow some vegetables*

Buy some vegetable seeds or seedlings
to plant. These could be for the garden
or they could be as simple as cress seeds
grown indoors. When they are grown, eat
them. As you eat them, enjoy them as fruit of
the earth and the work of human hands –
your own hands.

> **Think about this**
> What do you own that is most important to you? This is a gift from God. Next time you pray, thank God for it.

Name............................................................................................................

Taken from *His Spirit is with us*, published by Kevin Mayhew.

# Keep a food diary

Keep a record of the food you eat each day. Write down the main ingredients in processed food – for example, crisps are made from potatoes, biscuits are made from flour, milk and sugar. Thank God for the food given to us.

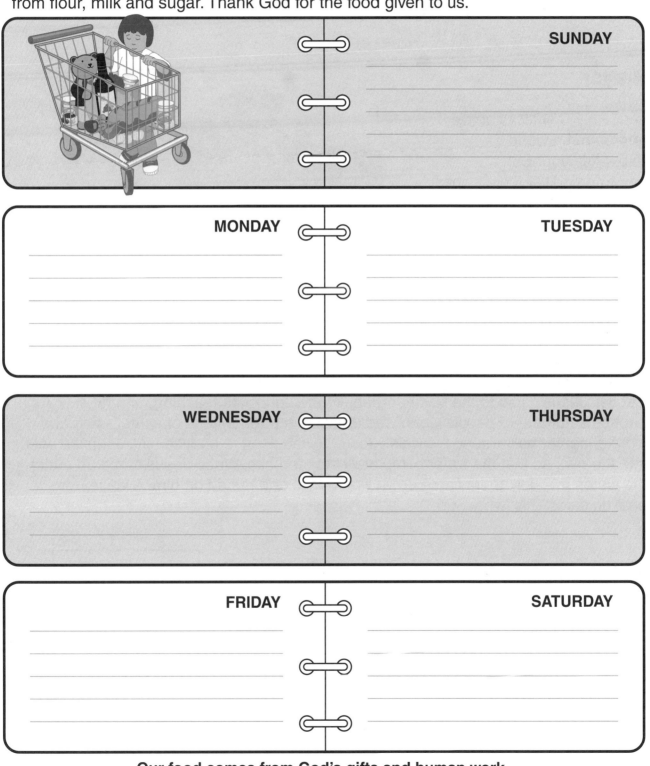

**SUNDAY**

**MONDAY**

**TUESDAY**

**WEDNESDAY**

**THURSDAY**

**FRIDAY**

**SATURDAY**

**Our food comes from God's gifts and human work.**

Name.................................................................................

Taken from *His Spirit is with us*, published by Kevin Mayhew.

# BIRD WATCHING

The Eucharistic Prayer begins like this:
  The Lord is here.
  **His Spirit is with us.**
This reminds us that the Holy Spirit is present at the eucharist, as well as at work in creation, in Jesus and in his followers. The Holy Spirit is often shown as a bird.

## Prayer
Almighty God,
your Holy Spirit was active
to create the world,
to baptise your Son
and to empower the disciples.
Strengthen us by your Holy Spirit,
to proclaim your praise
and to live to your glory;
through Jesus Christ our Lord.

## Bible story
### *The Holy Spirit at Jesus' baptism* (Matthew 3:13-17)
Before he began his work of teaching and healing, Jesus was baptised by John the Baptist. Jesus came to the River Jordan, where John was teaching, and he saw John baptise a number of people. John was dressed in a rough coat of camel's hair and wore a leather belt around his waist. Jesus asked John to baptise him. John led Jesus into the river so that the water completely covered him. When Jesus came up out of the water, the Holy Spirit came down like a dove and rested on him. A voice from heaven said, 'This is my Son.'

## To do with others
### *Feed some birds*
Remember that the Holy Spirit is often pictured as a bird. Learn more about birds by watching them. Invite them to your home with food. First plan which birds you wish to attract and then find out what food they prefer. Find or make a suitable feeding tray and choose a good location for it. Remember to keep filling it with food.

> **Think about this**
> What is there about birds that makes you think of the Holy Spirit?

Name.............................................................................................................

Taken from *His Spirit is with us*, published by Kevin Mayhew.

# A game to play

1. Cut out the cards. Shuffle them, give four cards to each player and put the rest face down.
2. Complete the verses by finding pairs and placing them on the table.
3. Player 1 takes one card from the pile. If this card makes a pair, this is placed on the table. Player 1 must put out one card, face up on a new pile. Player 2 can take the top card from either pile, placing any pairs on the table and discarding one card to the face-up pile.
4. Continue, using all the cards in your pile, then turn over the discard pile. Keep going until there are no more cards left. The winner is the player with the most pairs.

| | | |
|---|---|---|
| **The Spirit of God . . .**<br>GENESIS 1:2 | **(God said) I will pour out . . .**<br>JOEL 2:28 | **They were all filled with the Holy Spirit . . .**<br>ACTS 2:4 |
| **. . . was moving over the water**<br>GENESIS 1:2 | **. . . my spirit on everyone.**<br>JOEL 2:28 | **. . . and began to talk in other languages.**<br>ACTS 2:4 |
| **When the spirit came on them . . .**<br>NUMBERS 11:25 | **(God said) You will succeed, not by military might . . .**<br>ZECHARIAH 4:6 | **Those who are led by God's Spirit . . .**<br>ROMANS 8:14 |
| **. . . they began to shout like prophets.**<br>NUMBERS 11:25 | **. . . or by your own strength, but by my Spirit.**<br>ZECHARIAH 4:6 | **. . . are children of God.**<br>ROMANS 8:14 |
| **The Spirit of the Lord took control of David . . .**<br>1 SAMUEL 16:13 | **Jesus saw heaven opening and the Spirit . . .**<br>MARK 1:10 | **Surely you know that you are God's temple . . .**<br>1 CORINTHIANS 3:16 |
| **. . . and was with him from that day on.**<br>1 SAMUEL 16:13 | **. . . coming down on him like a dove.**<br>MARK 1:10 | **. . . and that God's Spirit lives in you!**<br>1 CORINTHIANS 3:16 |

**The Holy Spirit has been at work all through history and is present with us at the eucharist.**

Name...........................................................................................................................

Taken from *His Spirit is with us*, published by Kevin Mayhew.

The great shout 'Holy, holy, holy Lord' reminds us of the greatness and majesty of God. We are amazed by the vastness of outer space and by the greatness of the sun. We are even more amazed by the God who made the whole universe.

## Prayer

Holy, holy, holy Lord,
you are Lord of earth and sea,
you are God of sun and moon.
Holy, holy, holy Lord,
you are Lord of stars and planets,
you are God of all there is.
Holy, holy, holy Lord.

## Bible story

### The mighty sun (Psalm 19:1-6)

When the writer of the psalms looked up into the sky, he saw the sun, moon, stars and planets. It seemed that all these great lights in the sky were singing and shouting God's praises. So he wrote this great hymn of praise to God who made them all:

> The heavens above shout God's praises:
> the great lights tell out what he has made.
> The sun wakes up in the morning
> like a strong man ready to run his race.
> He rises at one end of the heavens,
> travels right across the sky
> and sets in the farthest west.
> Nothing is hidden from his light.
> The heavens above shout God's praises:
> the great lights tell out what he has made.
>
> (*from the* **Good News Bible**)

> **Think about this**
> When did you last make something like a model or some artwork? Think of all the time and work it took. Think of God's work that we see in the heavens and the earth.

## To do with others

### Count the stars

Go outside together at night. Look at the stars. Admire them. Try to count them. How many can you count? Look again and think about God who made them all. The stars show how great God is.

Name.................................................................................................

Taken from *His Spirit is with us*, published by Kevin Mayhew.

# A coded message

Decode this message. Use the letter grid to help you. Each letter can be found by looking at the code. If you need to find D2 you look along the bottom for column D, then go upwards to row 2 to find the letter is J.

As you find each letter, colour in that square. When you finish you will find the coloured letters make a special name.

```
E4  G3  A4  I1  K2  A1      F1  I4  E3      J1  G4  K3  A2  C4
```
                              ,
```
C2  E1  B4  G2      I3  C1  G1  I2      A3  E2  J4  B1  F4
```

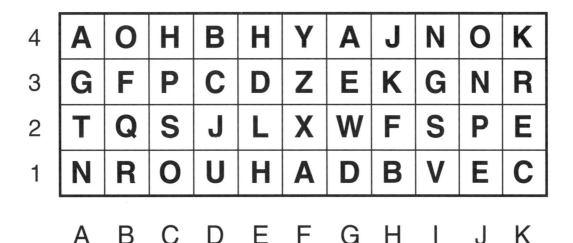

|   | A | B | C | D | E | F | G | H | I | J | K |
|---|---|---|---|---|---|---|---|---|---|---|---|
| **4** | A | O | H | B | H | Y | A | J | N | O | K |
| **3** | G | F | P | C | D | Z | E | K | G | N | R |
| **2** | T | Q | S | J | L | X | W | F | S | P | E |
| **1** | N | R | O | U | H | A | D | B | V | E | C |

A   B   C   D   E   F   G   H   I   J   K

**We praise God for God's greatness!**

Name...................................................................................................................

Taken from *His Spirit is with us*, published by Kevin Mayhew.

While celebrating the Passover meal with his disciples, Jesus gave a new meaning to the bread and to the wine. Every time the eucharist is celebrated we share with Jesus in that great meal.

## Prayer

Lord Jesus Christ,
at the Last Supper
you took bread and blessed it,
you broke bread and shared it.
As we do this in remembrance of you,
may we know your risen power in our lives
and share in your eternal kingdom,
where you live and reign
now and for ever.

## Bible story

### The Last Supper (Mark 14:12-16, 22-25)

The Passover is a great festival for the Jewish people. They meet together for a meal in the evening and as they eat the special food they tell the great tale of how God rescued them from being slaves in Egypt. Jesus arranged to celebrate the Passover meal with his 12 disciples in a large upstairs room. During the supper, Jesus took bread, he said the blessing, broke the bread and he shared it with the disciples. He said, 'Take this; this is my body.' Then he took a cup, said the blessing and shared it with them. He said, 'Drink this; this is my blood.' We repeat Jesus' actions and words at the Passover meal every time we celebrate communion.

## To do with others

### Remember Jesus

Jesus said that when we break bread and drink wine together we should remember him. We do this each week at the eucharist. But we can remember Jesus at other times too. Spend a meal-time remembering Jesus. Include bread as part of the meal. As you eat, tell each other your favourite stories about Jesus. Remember as many stories as you can. Finish by remembering stories of Jesus' death, burial and resurrection.

> **Think about this**
> We remember Jesus when we celebrate the eucharist. What other times help you to remember him?

Name...................................................................................................................

Taken from *His Spirit is with us*, published by Kevin Mayhew.

# Complete the table

Look for the ways in which our eucharist is like the Last Supper Jesus ate with his disciples. Tick the sections below.

|  | Last Supper | Eucharist |
|---|:---:|:---:|
| bread on the table | ✓ | ✓ |
| wine on the table |  |  |
| Jesus present |  |  |
| Jesus' followers present |  |  |
| people reclining at the table |  |  |
| people kneeling before the table |  |  |
| the bread is broken |  |  |
| 'This is my body' is said |  |  |
| the wine is poured |  |  |
| 'This is my blood' is said |  |  |

**When we celebrate the eucharist we remember Jesus' Last Supper.**

Name.................................................................................................................

Taken from *His Spirit is with us*, published by Kevin Mayhew.

# BREAD AND WINE

In the Acclamation we say:
**Christ has died:**
**Christ is risen:**
**Christ will come again.**
Here we proclaim our faith that Christ is present with us through the bread and wine.

## Prayer

Lord Jesus Christ,
we praise you for your gift of bread;
for seed time and harvest,
for sun and rain,
for miller and baker.
Lord Jesus Christ,
we praise you for the gift of yourself:
made known to us
in the breaking of bread.

## Bible story

### *Jesus shares bread with his friends* (Luke 24:28-32)

After Jesus rose from the dead on Easter Sunday, he met two of his disciples as they were walking along the road away from Jerusalem to Emmaus. They did not know Jesus had risen from the dead. They were sad and did not even recognise him. But because it was growing late, they invited this stranger to stay with them. When Jesus sat down with them for a meal, he took the loaf of bread. He said the blessing. He broke the bread and he shared it with them. In the sharing of the bread they recognised Jesus was with them. In the eucharist we, too, do those four things: we take the bread; we say the blessing; we break the bread; we share the bread. In the sharing of the bread we know that Christ has died, Christ is risen and Christ will come again.

## To do with others

### *Visit a bread shop*

Bread is important in our lives. Most of us eat bread every day. Bread is also important to us because of its use in the eucharist. Visit a bread shop and look at all the different types of bread on sale. Buy some bread that you have never tried before. As you eat it, remember how important bread is to us.

**Think about this**
Jesus promised that he would come again. This is one of the things we remember each week.

Name.....................................................................................................................

Taken from *His Spirit is with us*, published by Kevin Mayhew.

# Make your own bread

Bread is an important part of the eucharist. It is an important part of our lives.
Try making your own loaf of bread. You will need a hot oven, so first ask permission to use it.

### Milk loaf
### *Ingredients*

1 sachet dried yeast
450ml warm milk (body temperature)
6 cups (700g) plain flour
extra flour and milk

1 teaspoon sugar
50g butter
1/2 teaspoon salt

### *Instructions*

1. Rub the butter into the flour. Add the salt.
2. Add in yeast and sugar and enough milk to make a dough. Mix it with your hands.
3. Lightly dust flour on a table and knead the dough until it feels smooth and elastic.
4. Grease a clean bowl. Put the dough inside it. Cover the bowl with cling film and leave it in a warm place until the dough has doubled in size. (This can take between 30 minutes and 2 hours, depending how warm your chosen place is. A hot water cupboard is a very good spot. An oven is too hot.)
5. Lightly knead your dough again. Shape it into a round loaf. Place it on a greased oven tray.
6. Brush your loaf all over with milk. Put it in a warm place for 15-30 minutes until doubled in size.
7. Bake in a hot oven (400°F or 200°C) for 10 minutes and then turn the temperature down to moderately hot (375°F or 180°C) for another 15 minutes. (To tell if your bread is cooked, tap it gently on the side. It should sound hollow.)

**When we eat bread at the eucharist, we know Jesus is near.**

Name..........................................................................................................................

Taken from *His Spirit is with us*, published by Kevin Mayhew.

# CARNIVAL TIME

The Eucharistic Prayer concludes with a great shout of praise. Our celebration can be expressed as a carnival held in honour of the presence of the risen Christ.

## Prayer

Lord Jesus Christ,
you came into Jerusalem
riding on a donkey.
The crowds praised your holy name
and waved branches in the air.
Lord Jesus Christ,
you come among your people
in the bread and in the wine.
We glorify your holy name
and sing your praises for ever.

## Bible story

**The crowds welcome Jesus with palm branches (Matthew 21:6-11)**

On Palm Sunday Jesus rode into Jerusalem on a donkey to show the people that he was a gentle leader, not a war-like warrior. The crowds gathered around him and went wild with excitement. Some people took off their cloaks to make a royal carpet for him to ride on. Others cut branches from the trees to spread in his path. They all raised the shout, 'Blessings on him who comes in the name of the Lord.' We, too, can raise that shout of praise and wave our arms and banners when we meet with Christ in the eucharist.

## To do with others

*Visit a fair*

Why not celebrate together at a fun fair or carnival or theme park? Perhaps you could visit a local park together and enjoy the equipment and activities. At the end, talk about the things you most enjoyed. What a time of celebration! We celebrate like this in the eucharist.

> **Think about this**
> Our time in church is a time of celebration. It is a time to be joyful and celebrate that Christ is risen.

Name......................................................................................................................

Taken from *His Spirit is with us*, published by Kevin Mayhew.

# Make musical instruments

Use musical instruments to help you celebrate.

### Shakers
Choose a cardboard box with a tight-fitting lid.
Put a handful of rice inside it. Decorate the box.

For a different sound you could put the rice inside
a tin or a plastic container instead of a box. To put
a lid on the tin, use fabric or paper held in place
with a rubber band.

You can change the sound again by using macaroni
or pebbles instead of rice.

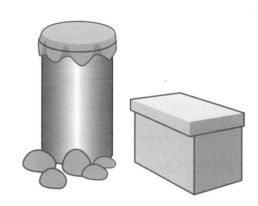

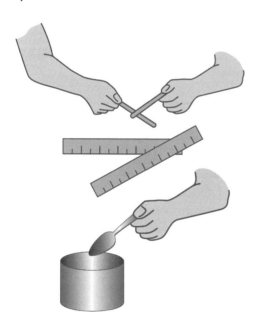

### Tapping sticks
Use two wooden rulers or two pencils to tap
together in time to the music.

Change the sound by tapping plastic sticks
together (for example, two long pieces of
Lego) or by tapping a metal spoon against
an empty tin.

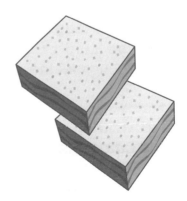

### Sandpaper blocks
Glue coarse sandpaper on to two blocks of wood.
Brush the blocks of wood against each other so
that the sandpaper pieces rub together.

**The Eucharistic Prayer is a time for celebration.**

Name.........................................................................................

Taken from *His Spirit is with us*, published by Kevin Mayhew.

The Lord's Prayer is the family prayer of the church. We pray this prayer together as a family just before we share in the family meal of the eucharist.

## Prayer

Lord God,
your Son Jesus Christ
showed us we belong to your family
and taught us to call you Father.
Help us to know your presence
as we share your family meal
of bread and wine;
through Jesus Christ our Lord.

## Bible story

### Jesus teaches his disciples to pray (Luke 11:1-4)

St Luke tells us that Jesus often spent time alone in prayer. His followers saw this and asked Jesus to teach them how to pray. They said, 'John the Baptist taught his followers to pray. Teach us how to do so as well.' Jesus answered like this. 'When you pray say:

Our Father in heaven,
hallowed be your name,
your kingdom come,
your will be done,
on earth as in heaven.
Give us today our daily bread.
Forgive us our sins
as we forgive those who sin against us.
Lead us not into temptation
but deliver us from evil.'

> **Think about this**
> The church is like a family, the family of God. We belong in the church.

Because Jesus taught this special prayer to his followers we know it as the 'Lord's Prayer'. Today we share this prayer with Christians throughout the world.

## To do with others

### Learn the Lord's Prayer

The Lord's Prayer is the family prayer of the Church. Communion is a special meal for the family of God. After your next family meal, say together the Lord's Prayer.

Name..............................................................................................................

Taken from *His Spirit is with us*, published by Kevin Mayhew.

# A family scrapbook

Begin a scrapbook about your family. Use photographs, drawings and writing. You could include sections about:

    people in my family
    what my family does
    things my family says
    places my family visits
    times my family celebrates

# A wordsearch

Hidden below are the words of the first part of the Lord's Prayer. The words go across, back, up and down (but not diagonally) and one word goes around a corner. Most words share letters with at least one other word.

Go through the prayer, crossing off the words one by one as you find them.

| B | E | F | O | R | G | I | V | E | A | R | T | H |
|---|---|---|---|---|---|---|---|---|---|---|---|---|
| E | V | I | G | N | O | H | W | W | ■ | U | S | ■ |
| B | I | ■ | K | I | N | G | D | O | M | O | U | R |
| R | G | C | O | M | E | S | R | U | O | Y | ■ | U |
| E | R | I | N | E | V | A | E | H | U | ■ | D | O |
| A | O | ■ | D | F | A | T | H | E | R | N | O | Y |
| D | F | N | A | M | E | S | A | B | E | I | N | A |
| N | L | L | I | W | H | A | L | L | O | W | E | D |
| I | U | S | L | E | S | O | H | T | O | U | R | O |
| S | I | N | Y | ■ | U | A | G | A | I | N | S | T |

Our Father in heaven,
hallowed be your name,
your kingdom come,
your will be done,
on earth as in heaven.
Give us today our daily bread.
Forgive us our sins
as we forgive those who sin against us.

**Write your own Wordsearch, using the rest of the words from the prayer:**
    Lead us not into temptation
    but deliver us from evil.
    For the kingdom, the power,
    and the glory are yours
    now and for ever.  Amen.

**The Lord's Prayer is the family prayer of the Church.**

Name...............................................................................................

Taken from *His Spirit is with us*, published by Kevin Mayhew.

## FAIR SHARES

At the breaking of the bread we say:

**Though we are many,**
**we are one body,**
**because we all share in one bread.**

We remember that Jesus shared food with the 5000 people. We, too, need to share our resources with God's people throughout God's world.

## Prayer

Eternal God,
your Son Jesus Christ broke bread
to feed a hungry people
and to bring new life
to a broken world.
When we break bread in his name,
fill us with his life
and send us out
to share his love with others.

## Bible story

### Food is shared among 5000 people (Mark 6:35-44)

Sometimes great crowds of people followed Jesus out of the towns and villages to hear him teach. One day the crowd had grown to about 5000. Towards the evening the disciples interrupted Jesus and said, 'It is getting late and these people are a long way from home. Send them off to get something to eat.' Jesus, however, told the disciples to see how much food they had to hand. They produced five loaves of bread and two small fishes. Jesus ordered the people to sit down on the green grass in groups of about 100. Then Jesus took the loaves; he said the blessing; he broke the loaves; he shared the loaves among the disciples; and he told the disciples to distribute the pieces to the crowd. Everybody ate to their heart's content and there was still some left over. In the eucharist we, too, share loaves of bread with Jesus and with all his disciples throughout the ages.

## To do with others

### Make a mural

Newspapers and magazines contain pictures and articles about people in need around our world. They also tell about people who have helped, and about groups that help people in need. Glue articles and pictures onto a large sheet of paper to display. Keep updating your mural with new articles.

**Think about this**
You own many things. Do you need them all? What do you have that you can share with others?

Name...............................................................

Taken from *His Spirit is with us*, published by Kevin Mayhew.

# Many yet one

A loaf of bread has many slices.
Is the loaf one thing or many?

A book has many pages.
Is the book one or many?

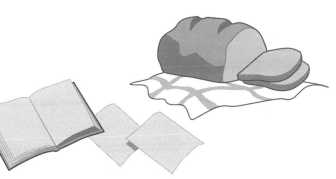

Some things are made up of many others. The many others are complete by themselves but when put together they make something different.

**Match the words and pictures below so that the many are joined with one.**

A letter has many

A school has many

A village has many

A team has many

A tree has many

A zoo has many

A house has many

A field has many

children

bricks

animals

ears of corn

words

buildings

players

branches

**Though we are many, we are one body
because we all share in one bread.**

Name..................................................................................................................

Taken from *His Spirit is with us*, published by Kevin Mayhew.

## PILGRIM WAY

We are invited to draw near with faith and to receive the sacrament. We respond by making a pilgrimage to the altar. There we meet with Christ in a special way.

## A prayer

Come, Lord Jesus,
stand among us in the bread and wine.
Come, Lord Jesus,
draw us near to your table.
Come, Lord Jesus,
live in us and stay with us.
Come, Lord Jesus, come.

## A Bible story

### Moses meets with God (Exodus 3:1-6)

When Moses was a young man he worked for his father-in-law Jethro as a shepherd. One day he was out with the sheep near Mount Horeb, which is known as 'the mountain of God'. Suddenly Moses noticed a bush which was on fire but which was not being burnt up. Looking at the bush Moses became aware that God was there with him and talking to him. He took off his shoes as a sign of reverence and covered his face because he was afraid to gaze on God. When we come to the eucharist, we know that God is with us in the bread and in the wine, just as Moses knew he was there in the burning bush. Like Moses, we want to draw near to God with reverence.

## To do with others

### Plan a pilgrimage

Find out about some places that are important to Christians, especially the places where Christians travel on pilgrimage. Choose one close to your home – for example, your local cathedral, or somewhere you visit on holiday. Work out some things you would like to see when you go there next time. (If you cannot make a real pilgrimage you can make one in your imagination. Borrow books about the place you would like to visit. Look at pictures and imagine what it would be like to be there.)

> **Think about this**
> You have heard about special pilgrims. You too can make a pilgrimage every time you visit the altar rail for communion.

Name.................................................................................................................

Taken from *His Spirit is with us*, published by Kevin Mayhew.

# A pilgrim's map

This is a map of the imaginary town of Balbourne. Imagine that many pilgrims come to visit. Special places of interest are marked by symbols. The people come to see:

the Norman church

the drinking fountain

the memorial statue

the display in the Town Hall

the Cathedral

Choose two other places for pilgrims to visit and mark them on the map with symbols. Now plan the best route through the town for the pilgrims to visit each place. Mark your route on the map. You may like to plan one route for people walking and a different route for those in a car.

**We, too, go on pilgrimage. When we go to the altar rail for communion or a blessing, this is a pilgrimage. We go to meet with Christ in a special way.**

Name............................................................................................

Taken from *His Spirit is with us*, published by Kevin Mayhew.

# BIRTHDAY INVITATION

The prayer, 'Most merciful Lord' reminds us that we are not worthy to eat crumbs under Jesus' table. Yet he invites each one of us to eat and drink with him.

## Prayer

Lord Jesus Christ,
you invite us to your table.
We are not fit even to eat the crumbs,
but your love welcomes us and draws us in.
Give us grace to accept your invitation
and to eat and drink with you,
in your eternal kingdom.

## Bible story

### Jesus eats with Zacchaeus (Luke 19:1-10)

Zacchaeus lived in Jericho. He was a Jew but had turned traitor by working for the Roman authorities. He collected taxes from the Jews to help pay for the Roman army. His fellow countrymen hated him. When Jesus came to Jericho, Zacchaeus, who was very short, climbed into a tree to see him. Jesus spoke kindly to Zacchaeus and invited Zacchaeus to eat with him. The crowds were shocked that Jesus shared a table with a man like Zacchaeus. We, too, are not worthy of Jesus' company, but Jesus specifically invites us to share his table.

## To do with others

### Design an invitation

Go together to a local stationery shop and look at all the invitations displayed – invitations to weddings, birthday parties, dinners, etc. Show each other your favourites. At home, design your own invitations. They are to be from God to your family, inviting you to join together at Jesus' table, to eat and drink with him.

> **Think about this**
> What is the most exciting invitation you have received? God's invitation for us to join together is even more exciting.

Name..............................................................................................

Taken from *His Spirit is with us*, published by Kevin Mayhew.

# Find your way

Receiving an invitation is only the first step to a party. The next step is deciding whether or not to accept.

Find your way through the maze, from the invitation to the party. Do not get side-tracked on the way!

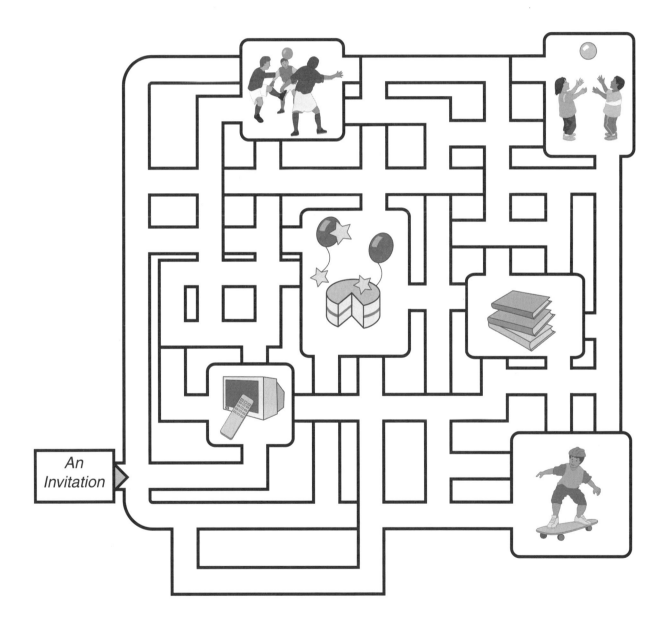

**We are invited to God's table each week.**

Name................................................................................................

Taken from *His Spirit is with us*, published by Kevin Mayhew.

# KNOWN BY NAME

When the bread of communion is placed in our hands, God is addressing us individually. God knows each of us by name.

## Prayer

Lord Jesus Christ,
you call us by name
to become your disciples.
We follow you.
Lord Jesus Christ,
you call us by name
to eat in your kingdom.
We praise you,
now and always.

## Bible story

### The birth of John the Baptist (Luke 1:5-25, 57-66)

Names are important to God. Here is a story about how one of God's prophets got his name. Zechariah was a priest who served God in the temple. He and his wife Elizabeth were getting quite old and were sad that they had no children. God chose them to be the parents of John the Baptist who was sent to prepare the way for Jesus. One day when Zechariah was in the temple, the angel Gabriel appeared to him and said, 'Do not be afraid, Zechariah; your prayer has been heard. Your wife Elizabeth will bear you a son, and you are to give him the name John.' When the child was born, everyone wanted to name him after his father and call him Zechariah. But Elizabeth and Zechariah spoke up. 'No,' they said, 'he is to be called John.' And it was so.

## To do with others

### Find out about names

Find a book telling the meaning of names. Use it to look up the names of everyone in your family. Does the meaning suit the person? Are there any other names with meanings that suit better?

> **Think about this**
> Even in a crowd of people, God knows you. God knows your name.

Name.................................................................................................................

Taken from *His Spirit is with us*, published by Kevin Mayhew.

# Make a stencil

Make a stencil of your name and use it to create your own writing paper.

**You will need**
  pencil
  card
  craft knife

writing paper
pencils or paint

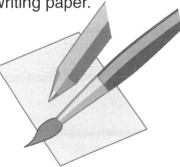

**What to do**

1. Practise first on a piece of paper. Print your name and then write around it to produce an outline that can be cut away. Remember that the whole letter will be cut out; you cannot leave spaces in letters like 'o' or 'a'.

**Sarah**

2. Copy the name on card and carefully cut it out using a craft knife. (If you have not used a craft knife before, ask an older person to help or to watch you.)

Sarah

3. Use the stencil to make your own notepaper. Hold the stencil firmly in place on a piece of writing paper and colour in the gaps. You can brush on paint or fill in the pattern with coloured pencils.

Sarah

**Your name is part of you.
God knows you by name.**

Name...............................................................................................

Taken from *His Spirit is with us*, published by Kevin Mayhew.

## COME DANCING

In the prayer after communion we thank God for feeding us in the eucharist. We offer to God our souls and bodies, our words and our dance.

## Prayer

Lord Jesus Christ,
we shout your praise;
accept our words.
Lord Jesus Christ,
we sing your praise;
accept our music.
Lord Jesus Christ,
we dance your praise;
accept our movement.
Lord Jesus Christ,
we live your praise;
accept our souls and bodies.

## Bible story

### *The healed man dances God's praise* (Acts 3:1-8)

Every day the crippled man was to be seen lying by the temple gate in Jerusalem, to beg money from those who passed by. He was so crippled his friends had to carry him there each morning. One day he saw the two apostles, Peter and John, and asked them for money. Peter replied, 'I do not have any money. But what I have I will give to you. In the name of Jesus Christ of Nazareth, get up and walk.' With that Peter helped the man to get up and the man found that he could walk. He was so excited he went into the temple with Peter and John, walking, leaping, dancing and praising God. After God's great gift to us in the eucharist, we too should say thank you with our whole being. And sometimes this can mean leaping and dancing as well as singing.

## To do with others

### *Dance*

Dancing is a joyful time. It is a time when we use our bodies to show how we are feeling. Think of all the things for which you would like to thank God. Put on some joyful music and dance your thanks together.

> **Think about this**
> After communion we offer God our souls and bodies. What could you do this week to use your body for God?

Name..................................................................................................

Taken from *His Spirit is with us*, published by Kevin Mayhew.

# Make up a dance

Choose a song or poem or psalm that says thank you to God. Create a dance or movement to go with it. You could use some of the movements below and make up some more of your own. Your dance could be for yourself alone or for you and a friend.

*Some movements to try*

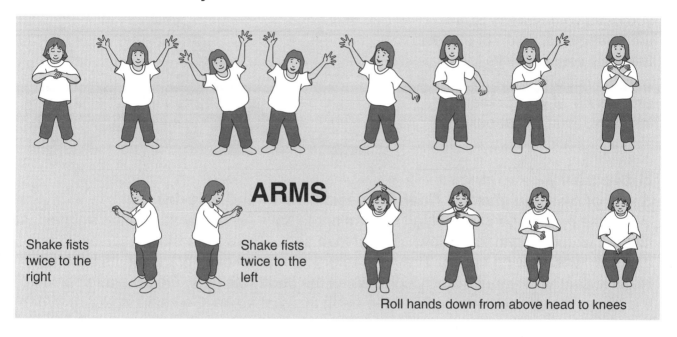

Shake fists twice to the right

**ARMS**

Shake fists twice to the left

Roll hands down from above head to knees

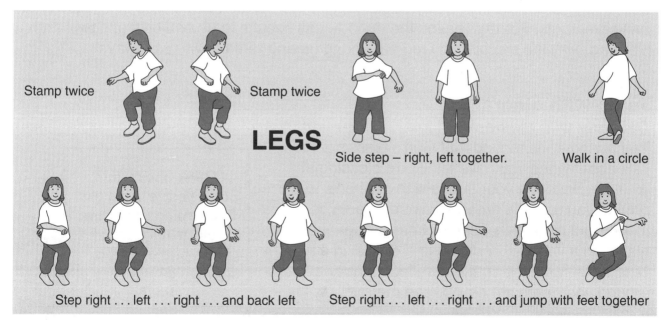

Stamp twice

Stamp twice

**LEGS**

Side step – right, left together.

Walk in a circle

Step right . . . left . . . right . . . and back left

Step right . . . left . . . right . . . and jump with feet together

**After communion we thank God for feeding us in the eucharist.**
**We offer to God our souls and bodies.**
**We can use our bodies to say thank you to God in dance.**

Name..................................................................................................

Taken from *His Spirit is with us*, published by Kevin Mayhew.

# RAINBOWS

The blessing at the end of the communion service pronounces God's favour and goodwill. We are reminded of the covenant God made with Noah when God placed the rainbow in the sky.

## Prayer
Lord God,
you gave your servant Noah
the rainbow as a sign of blessing.
Bless us your servants today
with the gift of your peace
and the joy of your presence;
through Jesus Christ our Lord.

## Bible story
### Signs of blessing given to Noah (Genesis 8:10-11 and 9:14-16)
When the great flood came, Noah built an ark to save his family and all the animals. At last the waters began to go down. Then Noah sent a dove from the ark to see if anything was growing nearby. The dove returned with an olive branch in its beak and Noah knew that dry land was in sight. When the flood was over, God put a rainbow in the sky as a promise never to flood the earth like that again. God said to Noah, 'When I put clouds in the sky above the earth, the rainbow shall be seen in the clouds. Then I will remember my promise. Never again shall the waters become a flood to destroy all living creatures.' For this reason the rainbow still speaks to us of God's goodwill and blessing. May the blessing of God be among us and remain with us always!

## To do with others
### Decorate with rainbows
The rainbow is a reminder of God's blessing. Talk about when you have felt God's blessing in your life. Decorate your house with rainbows to remind you of these times. A rainbow could be made from coloured paper, or from cellophane placed in a window, or suspend a crystal in a window to catch the light and reflect rainbows around your room. When you see the rainbow, remember afresh God's blessing.

> **Think about this**
> Some people use signs like a rainbow or dove to remind them of God's blessing. What sign could best remind you?

Name..................................................................................................

Taken from *His Spirit is with us*, published by Kevin Mayhew.

# Make a mobile

1. Make a large rainbow out of cardboard and coloured paper or pencils. (The rainbow is a reminder of God's blessing to Noah and to us.) The colours of the rainbow, in order, are red, orange, yellow, green, blue, indigo, violet.
2. Colour in the shapes below. Glue this paper on cardboard. Cut out the shapes. Draw any others you might want to add.
3. Use string or wool to suspend your shapes from the rainbow. Hang it in your room.

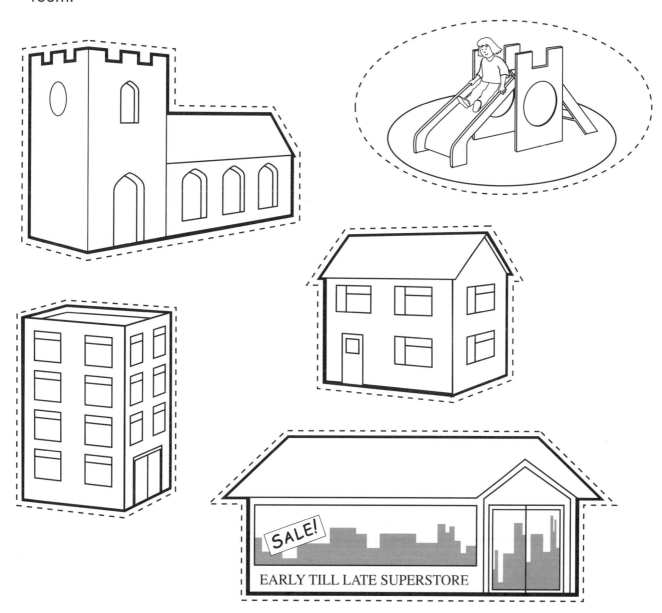

EARLY TILL LATE SUPERSTORE

**God's blessing is with us wherever we are.**

Name..................................................................................

Taken from *His Spirit is with us*, published by Kevin Mayhew.

# HELPING HANDS

The communion service ends with the Dismissal:
  Go in peace to love and serve the Lord.
This Dismissal sends us out into the world and tells us to set our faith to work.

## Prayer

Lord Jesus Christ,
send us out in your name,
to serve you by helping others.
Use our feet to run your errands;
use our hands to do your work;
use our eyes to show your love;
use our tongues to speak your words.
Lord Jesus Christ,
send us out in your name,
to your praise and glory.

## Bible story

***Jesus sends the 12 disciples out in his name*** (Mark 6:7-13, 30)
St Mark tells us how Jesus chose 12 people to be his special companions and disciples. For a long time these people followed Jesus everywhere he went. They listened carefully to what he said and watched closely what he did. Then Jesus sent these 12 disciples out in pairs to share his work and to do what he had been doing. When they came back they told Jesus all they had done and taught. At the end of the eucharist Jesus sends us out, just as he sent those 12 disciples, to carry on his work. Go in peace, therefore, to love and serve the Lord!

## To do with others

*Go for a drive*
At the end of the eucharist the dismissal sends us out into the world to love and serve the Lord. Think of the places you go to most weeks – for example, school, shops, work, playground, friends' homes. Visit these places. Begin at the church, ending back at your own home. Stop at each place and talk about how you can love and serve the Lord there.

**Think about this**
God wants us to love and serve him all week, not just on Sundays. How can you love and serve God at school?

Name.........................................................................................................

Taken from *His Spirit is with us*, published by Kevin Mayhew.

# Share a cake

**At the end of the communion service we are sent out into the world where our faith can work and grow and spread. Think of this as you prepare the cake below, as you watch it work and grow, and as you share the mixture with your friends.**

You will need to begin with a starter mixture. Your teacher or a friend might give you one, or you can make this yourself by mixing together: 2 teaspoons dried yeast, 1/2 cup lukewarm milk (body temperature), 1/2 cup plain flour and 1/2 cup sugar.

**DAY 1**
Add to your mixture:
 1 cup plain flour
 1 cup sugar
 1 cup milk
Stir well. Keep it covered but do not seal or refrigerate.

**DAY 2**
Stir.

**DAY 3**
Stir.

**DAY 4**
Stir.

**DAY 5**
Add to your mixture:
 1 cup plain flour
 1 cup sugar
 1 cup milk.
Stir well.

**DAY 6**
Stir.

**DAY 7**
Stir.

**DAY 8**
Stir.

**DAY 9**
Stir.

**DAY 10**
Divide your mixture into four parts. Use one part as the starter mixture to make the cake.
Give the other parts to three friends with a copy of this page.

**The cake**
You will need
 starter mixture (see above)
 1 cup of sugar
 1 cup of plain flour
 flavouring (see step 2)
 1/2 teaspoon of nutmeg
 2 teaspoons of baking powder
 1/2 teaspoon of salt
 1/2 teaspoon of cinnamon
 2 teaspoons of vanilla essence
 3 eggs
 1/2 cup of oil or butter

**What to do**
1. Mix together all your ingredients.
2. Fold into the mixture the flavouring of your choice –
   for example, mashed banana, grated apple, chopped nuts, crushed pineapple, raisins, grated carrot, coconut or whatever you would like.
3. Place the mixture into a greased cake tin, 20 cm (8 inches) square. Bake it for 45-50 minutes at 200°C (400°F).
4. If you wish, add the topping below.

**Topping**
 1/2 cup of soft butter
 1 cup of brown sugar
 1 teaspoon of cinnamon
 1 teaspoon of plain flour
Mix and spread over the cake.
Place under the grill for 5 minutes.

Name..............................................................................................................

Taken from *His Spirit is with us*, published by Kevin Mayhew.